Come See Where I Grew Up

A History of Piney Flats and Surrounding Areas

By:

Andrew D. Hare

ISBN: 1-4107-3056-5 (e-book)
ISBN: 1-4107-3057-3 (Paperback)

This book is printed on acid free paper.

1stBooks – rev. 06/14/03

Acknowledgements

There were many laughs when I told people about this project of writing a history of Piney Flats. Many believed that it was done entirely in vain, and that there was nothing significant enough that happened in our history worth remembering. I disagree with them on their assumptions. This project was done with the preservation of our heritage at heart. I believe that those that made Piney Flats what it is are true American heroes and they have been done an injustice by being forgotten over the last decades. It is my goal to try and preserve some of the precious memories of our past so that our children's children may enjoy the stories that shaped this community.

Thankfully there were many involved in seeing this project succeed. Ms. Janette Howze contributed greatly with historical documents, books, videos, audiotapes, and general knowledge of the area. My gratitude for her assistance is thoroughly appreciated. Johnny McKamey's stories of his childhood and documents were as valuable as gold to this projects completion. My Great-Aunt, Blanch Milhorn for opening up the past with her late husband's scrapbooks that included photos and documents of a forgotten time. Mark Mason bringing the glory of the 1950's and 1960's Mary Hughes Basketball teams back to reality. Duard Walker's valuable recollections of Mary Hughes football and community life of the 1930's. Written essays and documents by Michael Torbett, Nell Starnes, John Weaver, Lester Hyatt, and the late Lelia Hughes

Taylor and John "Squire" Anderson. All have preserved the rich history of this great community.

My middle school history teacher at Mary Hughes, the late Ms. June Hartsock, for inspiring my desire to learn history. Much of my knowledge about the history of Tennessee and this area was due to her efforts. I thank her for giving me a thirst to learn about my community.

There have been several efforts to preserve our local heritage in the past. Members of both Piney Flats and Bluff City communities in 1976 compiled the book, *Scenes From the Bluff,* and the work of Muriel Spoden and the Sullivan County Historical Society on their book in 1980, *Historic Sites of Sullivan County*, both proved valuable to my project. The work of the Holston Genealogical Society in their book *Families and History of Sullivan County, Tennessee Volume I 1779-1992*, became my grail in the final stages of this project. In March of 2000, the eight grade class at Mary Hughes led by Mrs. Becky Mason compiled a tour guide of Piney Flats titled, *Piney Flats Past to Present 8th grade Tour*. I am grateful for their efforts.

A very special thanks to my wife, Kelly Hare, sister, Krista Ivester, and sister-in-law, Beth Hare for their much needed editorial advice on this project.

Finally, everyone who made the history of my community so fascinating. I thank these men and women for their courage, vision, and strength.

Dedication

This book is dedicated to my wife, Kelly, for the patience, love, and support that she has given me in all of my pursuits. To my family, for teaching me to appreciate life and the lives of others. To GOD, may he be glorified in all of our actions.

Table of Contents

Chapter
One

A History of Piney Flats and Surrounding Areas

Piney Flats, Tennessee is located in the Forks Country of Sullivan County near the area where the Holston and Watauga Rivers join together. It has been my home my whole life and no matter where I go or where I will end up, Piney Flats will always be my home.

I remember growing up on Austin Springs Road and always asking questions to any one that would listen to me about the history of the area. The story of this wonderful community has and will always fascinate me. One thing I remember about all the questions I use to ask is no one seemed to know much about the complete history of Piney Flats. So it has always been a mystery to me how Piney Flats came to be. Once I got old enough to find things out for myself I discovered a great deal about the place I call home. It is because of this information that I decided to collect all I could find and put it together in one safe place.

Much has been written about the major landmarks of Piney Flats, New Bethel Presbyterian Church and Cemetery, Rocky Mount, Mary Hughes School, and the Devault-Massengill House. However, little has been written about the impact, as well as other sites, they had on Piney Flats. It is vital to the future of our nation that we do not forget about the story of our past. The history of our country will forever be documented however; it is the history of our homes and communities that are being forgotten. It is our responsibility to pass the torch of the past to the future generations so that they know where they came from. We

2

must give our children knowledge of where they grew up so that they will respect the land in which they live. Our fathers worked the land and sacrificed their time so that we may have a better life than they had. Let's pay the respect that is due to those who gave so much for the future and convince them that their efforts were not in vain.

Piney Flats is changing more each day. With every day that passes and every change made, another piece of what was once a bright and flourishing community fades away. The content of this book was obtained through oral traditions, books, essays, and church records.

It is my goal to put the pieces of the puzzle of Piney Flats together while giving you the answers to the questions I use to ask and to bring back the beautiful memories of a forgotten time.

There are actually three stories in the history of Piney Flats. First, we will learn the general history of Piney Flats. Which includes all the firsts; first settlers, first churches, first schools, and first industries. Next, we will look at the historic sites of Piney Flats. We will learn about places that are still around today and learn of their significance in the history of the community. Finally, we will learn the story of Piney Flats. Here we will find out some of the interesting facts that made Piney Flats unique from all other communities.

Come see where I grew up and learn the story of Piney Flats.

Before the formation of cities and communities in the area now known as Piney Flats, the Cherokee Indians ruled the land. The Indians used this land as hunting grounds and temporary settlements. Thousands of artifacts have been found throughout the region demonstrating the influence the

Cherokee's had on this area. In most valleys and open fields arrow heads and other artifacts can be found. One local legend is of an Indian burial ground located near the south bank of the Watauga River just east of Devaults Ford in Piney Flats. Some Indian artifact hounds have found this sacred place confirming the legend. According to Cox in, *A History of Washington County*, in 1950, several graves were found with its bodies buried in an upright position in the area near Austin Springs. Along with the graves were artifacts belonging to the deceased. Nevertheless, the influence the Cherokee Indians had on this area is well acknowledged.

It was in pursuit of these Native Americans that encouraged people to explore the area of East Tennessee. On May 17, 1673 James Needham and Gabriel Arthur along with eight Indians left Fort Henry, now Petersburg, Virginia on the James River in search of a passage through the Appalachian Mountains to the Indian villages of the Overhill Cherokees. They successfully made their way into present-day Tennessee going though Johnson County near Trade. They continued south and reached the Cherokee Nation along the Little Tennessee River. They became the first known Englishmen to cross the Appalachian Mountains. It is believed that the two explorers and their crew stopped at the spring at present day Tipton-Haynes Historic site in Johnson City. Here they could get clean water and have shelter for the night in the cave that is on the premise. However, there is little evidence of their stay in the Tri-Cities.

As settlements grew along the Eastern Seaboard, new immigrants to the "New World" continued west for their homes. Word had spread of the fertile valley across the mountains full of wildlife by way of Indian traders. Long Hunters, named so for their lengthy journeys while hunting game, would return to the settlements with stories of how plentiful the game was in this area. Rev. Samuel Hodges' Historical Sermon at the New Bethel Presbyterian Church's bicentennial celebration in 1882 said:

"Abundance of game gave them a fine range for pasturage yielding to imperfect cultivation, large returns and the magnificent forests were the natural inducements. Bancroft describes the valley of the Watauga and the surrounding regions as follows:

The health giving westerly winds prevail at all season. In spring the wild crab apple filled the air with the sweetest of perfumes. A fertile soil gave industry good crops of maize. The clear streams flowed pleasantly without tearing floods. Where the closest thicket of spruce and rhododendron flung their coolest shades furthest over the river, trout abound. The elk and red deer were not wanting in the natural parks of oak and hickory, of maple, elm, black ash and buckeye. Of quails and turkeys and pigeons there was no end. The golden eagle built his nest on the topmost ledge of the mountains, wheeling in wide circles far above the pines, or dropping like a meteor upon its prey. The black bear, whose flesh was held to be the most delicate of meats, grew so fat upon the abundant of acorns and chestnuts that he could be run down in a race of three hundred yards; and sometimes the hunter gave chase to the coward panther, strong enough to beat off twenty dogs and yet flying from one."

However, the king of England issued the Proclamation of 1763, which allowed settlements only to the crest of the Appalachian Mountains. Lands to the west of the line were Indian territories and settlers who dare cross the line would receive no protection from the Indians. This came as a result of the French and Indian War (1756-1763), which saw the massacre at Fort Loudoun in the Cherokee Country. Royal governments could not adequately defend settlers in the frontier. This did very little to keep the white settlers out of this new frontier. Jesse Duncan was one settler that disobeyed the royal order to stay east of the Appalachians. He became the example for all would be settlers that dared cross the Proclamation Line of 1763. In 1765, Mr. Duncan was near a hunting camp in present day Boones Creek when he was ambushed by a group of Cherokee warriors. After a short struggle the Cherokees had taken not only Duncan's scalp but they also took his life. This made Jesse Duncan the first white man killed by the Cherokees in our region.

William Bean is given credit to being the first permanent white settler in this new land. In 1769, he and his wife built a cabin at the mouth of Boones Creek where it joins the Watauga River. Their son Russell was the first white baby born in this new frontier. This land was explored before the Beans' arrived. Daniel Boone had blazed trails through the area earlier. The Daniel Boone Trail ran through Piney Flats near the Watauga River where present day Austin Springs Road now runs.

Photo by: Andy Hare
State Historical Marker of Jesse Duncan, first white man killed in this area

Daniel Boone's Trail Marker erected
by the Tennessee Daughters of the
American Revolution. (photo by, Andy Hare)

The newly settled land was divided up into four settlements. They were known as the Watauga, North Holston, Carter's Valley, and the Nolachucky. Combined, the four settlements were known as the Watauga Settlements. Piney Flats was part of the Watauga portion of the settlements.

When these early settlers arrived they believed they were in the Virginia Territory. After the boundary line was surveyed, they found that they were actually in North Carolina. This meant that they had settled into Indian Territory and their lands actually belonged to the Cherokees. The British Colonial Agents ordered the settlements to be disbanded and for them to move. Outraged by this decree, the settlers attempted to buy the land from the Indians. The Cherokees refused, but did agree to rent the land to the settlers for a period of ten years. This did not solve all their problems though. Their settlements were too far to be administered by the government in North Carolina. Therefore, law and order was difficult to maintain.

In 1772, the settlers met at Sycamore Schoals, in present day Elizabethton, and agreed to form their own government. The government became known as the Watauga Association and the laws were written in the Watauga Compact. The government provided for a court of five members, a sheriff and a clerk, and they followed the laws of Virginia, so far as these met the needs of the frontier. The Articles of the Watauga Association became the first written constitution, adopted by free and independent people in America.

In 1775, the Transylvania Purchase gave the frontiersmen all the land in which they were currently renting as well as all of present-day Kentucky and North Middle Tennessee for 2,000 pounds sterling and 8,000 pounds of other goods. The Transylvania Purchase became the largest private land purchase in the Americas. Virginia and North Carolina refused to recognize the frontiersmen's newly acquired claim. This would eventually lead to many conflicts between the frontiersmen and the Indians as well as the governments of Virginia and North Carolina.

The Transylvania Purchase was not well received by many of the Cherokees. Cherokee Chief, Dragging Canoe, and many others opposed bitterly giving up so much land. Indian raids will frequent the region during the next several years. One such raid happened to the founder of New Bethel Presbyterian Church. Near the time of the American Revolution, Samuel Doak's home was attacked by a war party of Cherokee Indians. Doak was away in Abingdon on business when the attack occurred. His home was nearly destroyed and his wife and infant child were forced to flee for safety.

The wife of William Bean was captured by the Cherokees and was to be executed. Nan-Ye-Hi, a.k.a. Nancy Ward, "the beloved woman" pleaded with the council to forgo their decision and allow Mrs. Bean to go free. Amazingly they agreed and Mrs. Bean was escorted back to safety in the Watauga Settlement.

The American Revolution left an impact on what became known as Piney Flats. Many residents of the this area fought for the independence of our country. Long's Fort was located where the Watauga runs into the Holston Rivers known as the Forks Country. We know that there were military movements through Piney Flats during this time. In the pension statement for William King, it states

9

that there were troops organized at the mouth of the Watauga just before the Battle of Long Island Flats on July 20, 1776. This tells us that soldiers from this area traveled through our area, maybe through your own backyard.

Another encounter during the time of the Revolutionary war occurred in the Forks Country. In 1777, Henry Massengill Sr. had built a meetinghouse for the Presbyterian congregation in the area, known as the "Massengill House of Worship." By 1779 hostilities ran high in the region because of the Revolution. Both sides felt adamant about which cause they believed. The local Tories disagreed with Massengill, as well as the others that attended the church and burned it to the ground.

In 1780, soldiers from our community stopped at Rocky Mount before crossing Devault's Ford on their way to muster with other soldiers at Sycamore Shoals for the Battle of King's Mountain. William Cobb supplied the men with horses, food, and slaves to aid them on their quest. The Battle of King's Mountain is considered by many to be the turning point of the American Revolution in the South. Without the help of this community the Revolution may have continued for several more years.

New Bethel Presbyterian Church, established in 1782,
is one of the oldest churches in Tennessee.

Photo by: Andy Hare

The American Revolution was not a war that occurred hundreds of miles away from what became Piney Flats. It was felt here with many of its inhabitants sacrificing their lives for our independence. The New Bethel Cemetery holds the remains of five Revolutionary War Veterans.

The Civil War was likewise felt here in Piney Flats. Tennessee was split with which side to take, eventually becoming the last state to secede from the Union. East Tennessee was divided, as well. With most of the area siding with the Union, Sullivan County, however, became known as "Little Dixie." No truer were the tales of brother against brother than here in East Tennessee. Many of the settlers of the area fought for whichever side they believed was right. In New Bethel Cemetery, graves of both Union and Confederate Soldiers can be seen.

Piney Flats saw little if even any conflict during the Civil War however; to the north in Bluff City several conflicts arose. Most famous was the Carters Raid in which the bridge crossing the Holston River was destroyed. In the Enterprise community, formerly referred to as Jeter's Mill, many homes along the Watauga River were searched and ransacked by Union soldiers, but no battles were fought. Troops undoubtedly did maneuver through Piney Flats but no support to any altercation can be found.

Through all of these events, what is now known as Piney Flats has seen it all. This area had given its all to make the United States a great country. Piney Flats has had some of its own die in the Civil War, WW I, WW II, and Vietnam. This small area has been a part of some large events. All of these events tie together in the shaping of Piney Flats. Every major event this country has seen, Piney Flats has been in the middle of it. The Watauga Association, the

Battle of Long Island Flats, the Battle of King's Mountain, Rocky Mount and the Southwest Territory, War of 1812, Mexican American War, Civil War, Spanish- American War, WW I, WW II, Korea, Vietnam, and Desert Storm all have been impacted by the area where I grew up, Piney Flats.

Sources:
Holston Territory Genealogical Society. Families and Histories of Sullivan County, Tennessee Volume One 1779- 1792. Waynesville, NC: Walsworth Publishing, 1992.

Rothrock, Mary U. This Is Tennessee. Knoxville, TN: M.U. Rothrock.

Spoden. Muriel C. Historic Sites of Sullivan County. Kingsport, TN: Kingsport Press, 1976.

Andrew D. Hare

Chapter
Two

Piney Flats

There has been several "histories" written about Piney Flats over the years. Mr. John Anderson wrote, "Historical Dates and Items of Interest on Mary Hughes School, and Town and Community at Large," on January 17, 1945, Mr. Michael Torbett wrote his paper at Mary Hughes titled "History" on May 9, 1966, Mrs. Lelia Hughes Taylor wrote "Piney Flats" in December of 1978, and Mrs. Nell Starnes wrote a section about Piney Flats for the *Families and History of Sullivan County, Tennessee Volume One 1779-1992*. All have formed the base for this section of the history of Piney Flats.

Piney Flats has changed greatly over the years. The Forks Country served as the name of the area from the 1770's to the late 1850's. There were several families that lived throughout the Forks Country on large farms that scattered throughout the countryside. The area that became Piney Flats was probably first settled by David Hughes. Hughes, originally from Ireland, settled the area in the late 1770's. He served twenty-one months in the American Revolution for a variety of commanders, including Isaac Shelby and John Sevier. Henry Colbaugh, an immigrant from Holland, received a land grant for an area in 1782. He built a log house that stood about a mile from where the train depot once stood.

In the 1840's, pioneer preacher Andrew Shell (1797-1880) settled the area. Until the coming of the railroad and its depot, Piney Flats was given the name Shell's Crossing or Shell's Cross-road. Because of the abundance of native pine trees and the gradual slope of the land toward the Watauga River, Shell's Crossing became Piney Flats. Years before, hunters and woodsmen referred to this area as Piney Flats.

Along with the Andrew Shell family, other families that settled the area were the Wolfes, Hughes, Massengills, Millers, Milhorn, Fords, Torbetts, Alisons, Kings and Smiths. Many of their descendants live here today.

Religion and Education was very important to the early settlers of Piney Flats. In 1777, Henry Massengill built the "Massengill House of Worship," The Presbyterian Church served there for two years until it was destroyed in 1779 by an invasion by Tories. This congregation contributed greatly to the organization of New Bethel Presbyterian Church in 1782. Samuel Doak, the first Presbyterian preacher and teacher in Tennessee, served as the first pastor. The church doubled as a school, and became the first organized school in Sullivan County. Rev. Joseph Rhea, who died before making the trip, organized the first real congregation of New Bethel in Maryland and Pennsylvania. The Cemetery at New Bethel holds the remains of many of the early settlers of the area, including a grave of the "Unknown Traveler" marked "I.G.-D.1790."

Shell's Chapel (named for Andrew Shell who donated the land for the church) was built in 1873 and also served as a school. Reverend Lucas, an English gentleman, was the first pastor and George W. McKamey the first teacher. In *History of Piney Flats United Methodist Church* records dating back to 1878 reveal the Sunday-to-Sunday activities of the Sunday School, including noisy children, selections of "singing books," appointment of a "begging committee," attendance of "visitors and deadbeats," wearing the usual "badge of mourning" for three months, and knife-trading in the church. The Union Church was established in 1913 with Rev. James P. Doggett, Presbyterian, preaching the first sermon, and Rev. J.M. Crow, a Methodist, preaching the dedication sermon in 1914.

Families and History of Sullivan County describe two little known churches of Piney Flats, the German Baptist Brethren and the Lutheran Dutch Church. The "Dunkard" or the German Baptist Brethren Church, which stood on the site of A.D. Browder's rent house across from Mary Hughes School. S.D. Hughes deeded the land for the church to the church in 1897. On certain Saturday evenings they would have a "soup eating and foot washing." Inspired by the chant like rhythm of the songs, the members would become highly emotional and kiss each other. Most of the members were poor but were recognized as "good people." They dressed in very plain clothes and wore no jewelry. The minister there was a Mr. Garst.

The Lutheran Dutch Church is also believed to have existed in Piney Flats during the early 1800's. The church was known as Gum Springs Meetinghouse but the exact location is not known.

Marker recognizing S.D.
and Mary Hughes for their
donation of land for the
future Mary Hughes School.
(photo by: Andy Hare)

Photo By: Andy Hare
Mary Hughes School located on Austin Springs Road.

The cornerstone for the Piney Flats School was laid in 1895, the Board of trustees met in 1896, and classes started in 1897. Samuel Hughes, who died before the school was completed, donated the land for the building of the school. The school was then named Mary Hughes in honor of Samuel's wife. Tuition for Mary Hughes Institute was $1 per month for grades 1-4, $1.25 grades 5-6, and $2 for special subjects. Subjects taught included algebra, plane geometry, rhetoric, civil government, philosophy, trigonometry, solid geometry, Latin, piano, voice, and elocution. Mae Sanders, Maude Sanders Bowman, Gertrude Sanders Ford, and Myrtle Sanders Grant served as some of the early teachers. In 1923 Mary Hughes became an accredited 4-year high school.

There are several important historic sites in or near Piney Flats, one of them being Rocky Mount. Rocky Mount was the home of William Cobb and served as the first capital of the Southwest Territory. William Blount served as the first Governor and established the seat of government at Rocky Mount from 1790- 1792 when the capital was moved to Knoxville. Devault's Ford, three miles north of Piney Flats marks the location where the Over the Mountain Men crossed on their way to fight the Battle of Kings Mountain.

An Indian trader named John Sharp built the first Mill in Piney Flats. It was a small tub-mill that stood at the mouth of Muddy Creek. J.M. King owned the first store in Piney Flats. Produce, cloth, and hardware were obtained at the King store.

The first telephone system in Piney Flats was built and partially owned by John Bunyan Wolfe and his brother William Wolfe. With a desire to communicate with the outside world, Mr. Wolfe built his own phone company with eight lines. The switchboard was located in the home of William Wolfe, with his wife, Margaret, serving as operator. He later joined with The Bluff City Phone Company, owned by James Henry, and E.T. Buckley of Rocky Springs to form the Holston Telephone Company. The Wolfe family bought out all the shares in the company and was sole owners until 1926. The Postal Telegraph and Telephone Company of Bristol purchased it with the stipulation that customers in Piney Flats would never have to pay long distance rates for calls to Bristol; this stipulation is still honored today.

Piney Flats also gave itself the distinction as being the smallest village in the world with its own power plant. The Piney Flats Electric Light and Power Company was established in 1918. The Piney Flats Electric Light and Power Company was a rarity for rural areas during the 1910's. This service gave residents of Piney Flats the luxury of electricity well before most surrounding areas.

In addition to his connection to his telephone and light companies, Wolfe started the Wolfe Brothers Furniture Factory in 1880, which employed between 30-40 workers.

The first train depot in Piney Flats for the Southern Railroad Company was built circa 1858. In 1900, a new depot was built across the track. Not all owners of livestock had sufficient land to graze their animals, so they allowed their cows to graze freely along the roadside and train tracks. Occasionally one would be on the tracks when a train came around the bend and the animal would be killed. The railroad would compensate the owners up to $12 for the killed animal. In attempting to be paid for a cow killed by a train, Mrs. Calbough found her efforts ineffective. She swore to get even and was able to do so by greasing the track on a steep grade behind her house. When the engine could not make the grade, the cow was paid for.

The first post office was located in the home of the first postmaster, Andrew Shell, whose five year receipts (1855-1860) totaled $20.01.

The first doctor in Piney Flats was Dr. M.M. Martin who also ran a store near his home. The second doctor was Dr. William T. Newton, the third E.M. Fleenor, and the last doctor was Dr. Aaron Cole.

Dr. Cole became a doctor in 1916 and served Piney Flats from 1925-1960. During his 44 years of practicing medicine, Dr. Cole delivered nearly 6,500 babies, including my mother. Due to the poor roads of the area, Dr. Cole road horseback when making his house calls. He continued this practice until the mid-1930's. Dr. Cole was one of the last true country doctors. He would understand if you could not pay your bill right away and would even accept items made by the patient if they did not have any money. His memory continues through the lives of the thousands of people he treated throughout his lifetime.

The Piney Flats Community Center (top) and the Fire Hall (bottom) were both built by the efforts of the Piney Flats Ruritan.
(Photos By: Andy Hare)

Other businesses in early Piney Flats were a livery stable, blacksmith, a "hoop factory"-manufacturing barrels of wood and hoops from the bark of certain trees, machine shops, a canning factory, and a place to pack feathers.

Since the time of the early pioneers, Piney Flats has received a total face-lift. The area in which this village originated is now home to several families now with all its original business and industry gone. The Post Office has been moved to U.S. HWY 11E, which is where the majority of the population has moved. Wolfe Furniture Factory, Ford's Canning Factory, the Blacksmith Shop, the General Stores, and the Train Depot are all a distant memory to those who remember Old Piney.

Lester Hyatt wrote a fitting poem about the changes in Piney Flats, especially since the Depot was torn down:

"There was Ford's Canning Factory
And Dow Mawks Black Smith Shop
And Wolfe Furniture Factory that made up
The industry of the town
When Piney Flats was a booming place.
Now they've tore the depot down.

There was Hugh Hawk and Big Alec Massengill
And Sib Ray all had General Stores
And Daddy Hawks store that stood on the edge of town.
Now Piney Flats just ain't the same
Since they've tore the depot down.

They have a new post office now
With a drive that goes All the way around.
The old post office is gone also,
Now they've tore the depot down.

There was Jim and me and Harry Ford and
Stoksie Bear and Mart and Press Frye
We liked to go to the station And watch the train go by,

And Harry Hendrix, the station agent who
Never wore a frown.
But Piney Flats just ain't the same
Since they tore the depot down.

We lived beyond the Huffman hill
About three miles from town
our old house is long since gone,
Now they tore the depot down.

I drove back one day to take a look At the old homestead,
Where we lived and worked so hard,
But all that was left of the old home place
Was the old apple tree that stood in the yard.

The old road is still there that leads over
The hill that brings you into town,
But Piney Flats just ain't the same
Since they've tore the depot down.

There was Bushy Miller, Peg Leg Jim's boy
That played the harp,
As the crowd would gather round.
He's gone, too, with all the rest,
Now they've tore the depot down.

The Dunkard church that stood
On the corner with the grove in back,
Where we would have dinner on the ground,
A dwelling house now stands in its place,
And they've tore the depot down.

In the cemetery in the back of the church
That stands upon the hill,
There lie the townfolks of yester years,
Their voices now are still.
They've reached the end of life's journey here
Their burdens they've laid down
Piney Flats ain't the same since they are gone
Now they've tore the depot down."

25

The New Piney in considerately different from the one Mr. Hyatt described. However, it is one that its people can be very proud of. Piney Flats has become somewhat of a mini boomtown. There are now over sixty businesses located within Piney Flats. They range from clothing and bicycle shops to sub-sandwich shops and barbecue restaurants. There is the Tri-County Industrial Park that boasts dozens of industries that proved hundreds of jobs to our region. Piney Flats has the Piney Flats Plaza that offers local residents the luxury of a grocery store, video rental, general store, Pharmacy, variety shops and restaurants all in one location. Yes, Piney Flats has finally caught up with the other communities in the region. Some people like the changes; others wish their little hamlet had stayed the same.

In Piney Flats today, there are several businesses that have succeeded in making the community of Piney Flats one that can be easily distinguished. In it's early years the major businesses of Piney Flats consisted of the train depot, Wolfe Brothers Furniture Company, Piney Flats Electric Light Company, The Holston Telephone Company, specialty shops, and several general stores. None of which are in existence today. When the winds of change swept through Piney Flats, the types of businesses and their locations changed with them.

Today the business and industry is now located on and around U.S. Highway 11E. The need to travel through Main Street was no longer necessary since a quicker and more direct road was now built. Thus the reason for the move of the heart of Piney Flats.

The nature of businesses, likewise, changed when the central location of Piney Flats moved. No longer were "mom and pop" general stores and services needed since a drive to Johnson City or Bristol was now an easier commute. Most of the businesses in Piney Flats are part of larger franchises that are all recognized everywhere throughout the country. However, there are several family ran businesses that have succeeded and became very successful throughout the region. It is people like these that have kept Piney Flats on the map and helped maintain its identity.

No one can travel through Piney Flats without recognizing the famous barbecue restaurant Pardner's Bar-B-Que and Steak Restaurant. Whenever I had to meet someone from outside of Piney Flats, Pardner's would always be the rendezvous point. Everyone knew where it was. Paul Bare, the brainchild of Pardner's, has been fixing fine meals for people from all over the country for over twenty years. During race weekends, forget about getting a table unless you don't mind waiting. It is always a popular "oasis" for weary race fans from other parts of the country, as well as drivers and crew of many of the Nascar teams. Throughout the rest of the year it is just as popular a place to eat for the natives. I have never driven by Pardner's when the parking lot was not at least half full.

Pardner's has been an icon for Piney Flats since the early 1980's. It has quickly become one of the most recognizable restaurants in Tri-Cities. They not only provide a quality environment for dining, they have a reception hall, and cater any event. Piney Flats is proud to call Pardner's it's own. Many others and I are thankful for it's good food, good service, and did I mention good food?

Photo By. Rene Rutherford
The Wolfe Brothers Furniture Factory, now no longer operating, was a major source of employment for the people of Piney Flats nearly eighty years.

Equally as recognizable in Piney Flats is Miller's Outdoor Center Inc. Miller's is a refuge for the outdoorsman and cowboy. Miller's was built and is operated by Danny Miller and has rapidly become one of the most respected outdoor businesses in the region. With much of their business done from consumers throughout the Tri-Cities, Miller's Outdoor Center is a very popular place. From cowboy boots and western wear to the finest hunting equipment; Miller's has it all.

Miller's, formerly called Miller's Archery, has been part of Piney Flats since the early 1990's. It has grown tremendously over the years having expanded several times. They have been responsible for the increased interest in rodeos in the area, sponsoring several rodeo competitions throughout the years.

If you're in the right circles, just mention Miller's Outdoor Center and chances are they will know exactly where it is. Miller's is one of the last true grassroots businesses that can call themselves a success. Piney Flats is truly grateful to have them as their own.

One cannot travel through Piney Flats without noticing all of the greenhouses. Several families in the community are involved in the greenhouse business, but one family stands above the rest. According to Janie Torbett in *Families and History of Sullivan County, Tennessee Volume One 1779-1992*, the Torbett family has been involved in the greenhouse industry since the early 1900's.

Pioneered by Eli Anderson Torbett (1876-1961), he became the forerunner of today's plant growing industry. This industry has been very successful over the years and continues to flourish today.

Today the third generation of Torbett's run and operate the greenhouses in Piney Flats. Most of their plants are sold locally or within the southeast. The greenhouse business has been a passion for the Torbett family having withstood the strains of depression, war, and community transition. And through it all the vision of Eli Anderson Torbett has survived nearly a hundred years to see his idea succeed today. Piney Flats and greenhouses, I can't imagine one without the other.

There are other businesses that deserve recognition as Piney Flats icons. Hodge Electric has served Piney Flats and the Tri-Cities for a number of years. Bill Hodge, owner, has provided many opportunities for people in the community to work and gain experience in the electrical trade. His contributions to Mary Hughes and the community cannot be measured nor appreciated enough. Piney Flats is truly gratefully for Mr. Hodge and his business.

No community would be complete without a place to loaf. Several gas stations in Piney Flats through the years have severed the role as the popular loafing spot for the community's professional loafers. Aside from getting your tank filled up, a cold drink, and a sandwich from the deli you can also enjoy some wonderful conversation from the loafers. Now these men do more than loaf, they all have jobs. It is just nice to know that there are still a few people left in the world that can stop and smell the roses and enjoy a cold drink with some friends. The great part about Piney Flats is that there are plenty of gas stations to do your loafing. As of 2003, there are four gas stations within a mile stretch of highway 11E.

The Piney Flats Ruritan, organized in 1954, has been instrumental in making Piney Flats what it is today.

Through its contributions and hard work, Piney Flats now has its own Community Center, Volunteer Fire Department and meeting area, and Community

Park and Softball Field. In addition to these improvements to Piney Flats the Ruritan contributed to the development of the Industrial Park, it supports the Boys Scouts of America, Piney Flats Volunteer Fire Department, Little League Baseball, Senior Citizens Groups, scholarships to a graduating senior from Piney Flats, recognizes academic excellence with an awards banquet for Mary Hughes Middle School and Sullivan East High School students, and many other projects.

Churches are a significant factor in the development of a community. The church offers not only a place of worship, but it is a place of fellowship, comfort, and safety. Piney Flats has long been a very religious community offering freedom to its citizens the right to choose their own faith. Piney Flats has a large number of churches with different denominations. There are three Methodist, two Presbyterian, a Christian/Church of Christ, a Church of GOD, a Baptist, a Free Will Baptist, and a Non-Denominational Church. All in an area of about five square miles. Piney Flats has always been a very religiously tolerant community. From the Dunkard Church to the Union Church where three denominations (Presbyterian, Methodist, and Baptist) of churches met, Piney Flats allowed the Constitutional right of Freedom of Religion to be practiced.

Beginning in the mid-1980's, Johnson City, Bristol, and Bluff City began actively seeking interest in the valuable location of Piney Flats. Through years of legislation Bluff City and Johnson City now lay claim to much of the right of

31

way on U.S. HWY 11E that runs through the heart of Piney Flats. These annexation battles have caused mixed emotions among the residents of Piney Flats. However, because of the annexation Piney Flats has become more accessible for business and industry to move into the area. On the other hand, most of the once pristine farm land and forests are quickly becoming a distant memory. Progress has a price and much of the progress of the area was unwanted. Nevertheless Piney Flats has grown tremendously since the annexation wars began. There is a large amount of new faces that have moved into the area. Residential growth has increased dramatically with the old family farms being sold and broken into lots.

Through all that has happened Piney Flats has lost a lot of its identity. More and more people have forgotten what a great community Piney Flats once was. Even with the signs marking Johnson City and Bluff City City Limits across the road from each other at the crossroads, the people of Piney Flats need to hold on to their heritage.

The best description I have ever heard about Piney Flats are in the words of Michael Torbett's essay on Piney Flats written over thirty years ago, "Times and prices have changed in Piney Flats. Rumor had it that Mr. Shell traded 100 acres of land for a rifle and a gallon of whiskey and another man traded his wife for a shovel plow. But the tribute found in the first catalog of Mary Hughes is still applicable: "Its people are hospitable, generous, and pleasant."

Chapter

Three

Rocky Mount

Rocky Mount, built by William Cobb between 1770-1772 is located in Piney Flats near the Sullivan County Washington County line. This two-story house of white oak was given its name for the limestone outcrops that are along the hillside. The nine-room house was very impressive by frontier standards. The white oak was cut from forests near by, the interior was pine paneling, and the glass windows were all rarities on the frontier. The main portion of the house is connected to the dining room by a "dog-trot," with its sides open to enhance summer breezes. Today Rocky Mount is a Tennessee State historic Site and on the National Register of Historic Places.

The kitchen is a separate building located a few yards from the house. The outbuildings, including the barn have been reconstructed. The barn was a stage change on the stagecoach road from Baltimore to Memphis.

On May 26, 1790, President George Washington signed an act establishing the Territory of the United States South of the River Ohio (commonly referred to as the Southwest Territory). President Washington appointed North Carolinian, William Blount, as Governor and Superintendent of Indian Affairs. Daniel Smith became Secretary; John Sevier was appointed Brigadier General of the eastern, and James Robertson for the western section. There were three judges of the Superior Court, David Campbell, Joseph Anderson, and John McNairy.

In October 1790, Governor Blount made Rocky Mount the Capital of the Southwest Territory. It remained the capital for 18 months until the capital was moved to Knoxville. Making Rocky Mount the first territorial capital west of the Allegheny Mountains and the oldest territorial capital standing on its original site.

Governor Blount found his choice of the capital very satisfactory. He wrote about his new home: "On the 11th instant, I arrived in this country, and was received with every mark of attention and gladness that I could have wished, I am very well established with a Room with Glass Windows, Fireplace, etc., etc., at this place."

Rocky Mount served Governor Blount as a law office and as a courtroom during bad weather. On nice days, court was held under a large white oak tree that stood beside the house.

Historical Marker by the Tennessee Historical Commission recognizing Rocky Mount and it's historical significance. (Photo by: Andy Hare)

I A   7
ROCKY MOUNT

300 yards to the southeast is the home of William Cobb, pioneer. First seat of government of the Southwest Territory. October 10, 1790; Governor William Blount had headquarters here till removal to Knoxville, the new capital, in 1792. Andrew Jackson lived here six weeks while waiting for a license to practice law.

(Photo By: Rene Rutherford)
Rocky Mount Historic Site. Home of William Cobb and Capital of the Southwest Territory.

Governor Blount came to Rocky Mount with instructions to solve the conflicts between the Cherokees and the white settlers. His job was to satisfy upset settlers and help them understand the Indians point, as well as to satisfy the grievances of the Indians.

The frontier's most prominent citizens knew William Cobb. However, unlike his constituents he steered clear of most political positions. Nevertheless, he served his country and region well in his efforts. In September of 1780, 950 frontiersmen gathered at Rocky Mount en-route to Sycamore Shoals and King's Mountain. Cobb provided the company with rations, gunpowder, horses and slave labor, in preparation for this Revolutionary War encounter (considered by many to be the turning point of the Revolution in the South).

Andrew Jackson spent six weeks at Rocky Mount while waiting to obtain his license to practice law in Jonesborough. After practicing law in Jonesborough, Jackson became the hero at the Battle of New Orleans and eventually our country's seventh President. Other to have visited Cobb at Rocky Mount was John Sevier (Tennessee's first Governor), famed trailblazer Daniel Boone, William Campbell, Richard Henderson, and Isaac Shelby.

Rocky Mount is now owned by the state, is administered by the Rocky Mount Historical Association, and can be visited seven days week for a small fee. A museum at Rocky Mount houses an extensive collection of historic collection of historic items from Upper East Tennessee. Among the approximately 15,000 artifacts are costumes and coverlets, early pottery and glassware, an unusual collection of toothpicks and ear spoons, and as exhibit of various lighting devices. The museum also has a number of historic manuscripts and documents and the original kettle in which Mary Patton made gunpowder at Sycamore Shoals for use at King's Mountain.

When you visit Rocky Mount, do not expect the guides to know what is happening in the world during the time of your visit. Rocky Mount is a living history museum and all its guides portray life in 1790. A visit today to Mr. Cobb's home is just as hospitable as it was over two hundred years ago.

(Photo By: Rene Rutherford)
Rocky Mount. Home of William Cobb from 1770-1795, Capital of the Southwest Territory 1790-1792, and a popular haven for many of Americas early leaders.

Andrew D. Hare

Rocky Mount continues to serve its country well for those that want a glimpse at a time when our country was in its infancy. It is a treasure to the heritage of our country and is a prize that Piney Flats is proud to call its own.

Sources:
Sakowski, Carolyn. *Touring The East Tennessee Backroads.* Winston Salem, NC: John F. Blair Publisher, 1993.

Spoden, Murial C. *Historic Sites of Sullivan County.* Kingsport, TN: Kingsport Press, 1976.

Devault-Massengill Plantation Houses One of the finest historic homes in Sullivan County, the Devault- Massengill Mansion is located on a small hill overlooking U.S. Hwy 11 E in Piney Flats. This home is built in a square of hand-fired brick with its windows bordered by white shutters. This well preserved home was built on one of Sullivan County's oldest plantations. Valentine and Frederick DeVault purchased the plantation in 1837 from Henry (Hal) Massengill Jr. It was Valentine's son, Isaac Devault who built the mansion in 1840- 1842. He directed the work from the old original Massengill slave cabin, having the bricks made by slaves on the grounds.

Isaac Devault's grandparents, Heinrich and Catherine Marie Graver Devault, were born in Paletine County, Germany in the Rhine River country. They immigrated to America in 1766 and settled in Pennsylvania where they died. Heinrich purchased a 637-acre tract of land from John Bean, which was located in Washington County, Tennessee, which he willed to his sons, Valentine, and Frederick DeVault. Their German heritage is obvious in the craftsmanship of the architecture in the home.

The Devault brothers moved to this area in 1800 and established the well-known Devault Place beside the old Jonesboro Road at Devaults Ford of the Watauga River south of the Massengill plantation. Valentine and Frederick Devault married sisters, Mary and Margaret Range and many of their descendants remain in Upper East Tennessee.

Isaac Devault and his heirs occupied his beautiful 385-acre Massengill plantation and brick mansion until it was sold out of the family to John Wexler. In 1937, one hundred years after it was sold out of the Massengill family, John M.

41

Massengill purchased the mansion and farm putting the old plantation back in the Massengill family.

One building from the old Massengill plantation remains on the property. A large cabin that the plantation overseer probably used is all that remains. In 1971, Sally Bachman had the hewed log cabin completely restored. This structure is the only remaining structure of the Henry Massengill plantation. The cabin's hand hewed shingles; flooring, stone chimney, hearth and fireplace are all unique. The door has a wooden hinge and latch of wood. There is a stairway that leads to a loft and the porch completes the original log house built by Henry Massengill in the 1770's.

(Photo By: Rene Rutherford)
Devault-Massengill Mansion. Original location of the Henry Massengill Sr. Plantation established in 1769. Today the house can by reserved for banquets, receptions, and reunions.

Andrew D. Hare

Henry Massengill Sr. (1740-1834) built this cabin near his three-story hewn log plantation house that burned in 1798. Henry Sr. came to the Watauga country in 1769, making him one of the first white settlers in Tennessee. Near the plantation, Massengill built the Massengill House of Worship in 1777. Unfortunately, while Massengill was away serving his country during the American Revolution, a group of disgruntled Tories burned the church in 1779. In all Henry Sr. had about 150 slaves and was one of the wealthiest men in the area.

In 1825, Henry Sr. sold the old place to his son, Henry (Hal) Massengill (1758-1837). Hal, like his father accumulated a large amount of wealth. Hal owned 1800 acres of land, had a wagon shop, hauled salt from Virginia, traded and freighted salt and other goods by flatboats to as far as Natchez, Mississippi. Hal as well as his brothers, Michael and Solomon, served as soldiers during the Revolutionary War.

Today the Devault-Massengill Mansion is just as impressive as it was over one hundred and fifty years ago.

Source:
Spoden, Murial. *Historic Sites of Sullivan County*. Kingsport, TN: Kingsport Press, 1976.

Henry Massengill and William Cobb

Henry Massengill and William Cobb are two men that are not only significant early settlers in present day Piney Flats but also their contributions have been felt all over the region.

Henry Massengill Sr. was one of the first permanent settlers west of the Appalachian Mountains. In 1769 he and his family moved to the area known as the Forks Country from the Meherrin River Valley in North Carolina. Henry was a very involved citizen of the area and instrumental in the formation of the Watauga Settlement.

On June 1, 1779 Henry wrote what he had accomplished in the early days of the frontier:

"In January 1772, I was with an illness which rendered me almost helpless for twelve months.

I was elected a member of the Watauga Association in 1775. But a return of my former illness prevented me from attending meetings until Sept., 1776. I entered upon active duty and served until 1777.

In April, 1777, Rev. Charles Cummings, a Presbyterian minister from Wolf Hills Settlement, came to Watauga and preached three days. We hailed his coming among us with great joy, for our souls were hungering and thirsting for spiritual nourishment. He urged the Settlers to build a house of worship, which we decided to do. I was to furnish logs, boards and all timbers needed to build a large house, with a section of benches in the backside for the Massengill and Cobb Negroes numbering at this time 151 souls. So these slaves can come out and be refreshed in body and soul. This house was completed by July, 1777, and was known as the Massengill House of Worship. Rev. Cummings and Mulkey preached several times to the Settlers.

I was chairman of a Committee of Safety for the Watauga Settlement, 1778. I was elected sheriff of Watauga District, served two years. I marched with Shelby against the Indians, 1779.

While I was away Tories came, abused my family, destroyed my property, burnt the Massengill House of Worship to the ground.

Written by Henry Massengill, Sr., Watauga District, this lst day of June, 1779."

Mr. Massengill had quite an impressive resume. He is one of our earliest settlers and his achievements are deserving of recognition even today.

William Cobb like Henry Massengill Sr. came from the Meherrin River Valley in North Carolina. He located in the Forks Country in 1770, a year after the Massengill's.

Cobb was a member of the first Washington County Court in 1778 and in 1780 was appointed "judges and viewers," of the currency of the realm. His name appears frequently in the records of the early Washington County records.

On August 7, 1790 President Washington appointed William Blount Governor of the new Territory South of the River Ohio. He reached the Watauga settlement the 10th day of October 1790, and in the absence of a special building, he selected the home of William Cobb as his headquarters to organize the territory. Making the Cobb home, Rocky Mount, and the first capital of the first recognizable government west of the Allegheny Mountains.

William was a very hospitable man always willing to entertain or lend a helping hand. J.G.M. Ramsey wrote this about Cobb in his <u>Annals of Tennessee</u>:

"Cobb was a wealthy farmer, no stranger to comfort and taste, not unaccustomed to what, in that day, was called style. Like the old Carolina and Virginia gentlemen, he entertained elegantly, without grudging. Like theirs, his home was plain, convenient, without pretension or show ... He kept his horse, his dogs, and his rifles, even his traps, for use, comfort and entertainment of his guests. His servants, his rooms, his grounds, were all at their bidding. They felt themselves at home, and never said adieu to him or his family, without the parting regret and tenderness of an old friendship."

During the Revolution, he aided the soldiers that were going to Kings Mountain with food and horses. His son Pharaoh Cobb, who lived farther up the Watauga River from William, also aided the troops and then joined them.

Shortly after the government of the Southwest Territory had moved out of his home, William sold his land in 1796 to his son-in-law. From 1795 to 1803 William lived in Washington County, Beans Station, Grainger County, and finally Knox County.

William Cobb gave his home for the building of our state and aided the soldiers that won us our freedom. His contribution are observed everyday at his home of Rocky Mount where you can go and see how important he was in the development of this area.

Sources:

Massengill, Samuel E. *Massengills, Massengales, and Variants 1472-1931*. Bristol TN: The King Printing Company, 1931.

Sakowski, Carolyn. *Touring The East Tennessee Backroads*. Winston-Salem, NC: John F. Blair Publishing.

Long's Fort Site

According to both *Historic Sites of Sullivan County* and *Families and History of Sullivan County, Tennessee Volume One 1779-1992*, a Revolutionary War fort was located at the confluence of the Holston and Watauga Rivers. Old records refer to it as Long's Fort.

Captain David Long who served in the Colonial Militia in this area may have built the fort. Captain Long moved out of the Forks Country between 1777 or 1778.

Micajah Adams, a Revolutionary War soldier, in his pension statement, named Long's Fort. Other pension statements of Cornelius Carmack and William King describe, "troops mustered at the mouth of the Watauga in a company commanded by Captain James Shelby just before the Battle of Long Island Flats which occurred July 20, 1776."

Robert Alison House

In 1779, Robert Alison came from Maryland to the Forks Country with his father, John Alison Sr. an Irish immigrant. Born in 1749, Robert was the eldest son of John and was a private with the Continental Army during the American Revolution and served under Colonel Theodore Bland. Robert married Martha McKinley, daughter of William McKinley Jr. who was President William McKinley's great-great-great uncle. The McKinley family emigrated to the area from Maryland about 1785.

49

In 1784, Robert received a 100-acre North Carolina land grant on the north side of the Watauga River. This marks the site of the home. Robert, a millwright and skilled carpenter, built his first home, which no longer stands, near the site of the present home. He gave his first house to his son Joseph as a wedding present. Robert then moved into his new home, which he built with hewn logs.

(Photo By: Rene Rutherford)
The Robert Alison House is located on the original 100 acre land grant given to Robert in 1784. This is the second home he built after he gave the original home to his son as a wedding present.

The house has two large cut-stone chimneys that are still in excellent condition. One of the several interesting features about the home is the small basement room. It contains a very large fireplace and a hand-fired brick floor. The only entrance to the basement was through an outside door. Today there has been an inside entrance to the unique cellar. The house is still in near original condition.

The house stayed in the Alison family until 1855. One of the later owners was Joe Milhorn. The home became known throughout the area as the "Joe Milhorn Place." My grandfather, Sam Milhorn, was born here and lived there until the 1930's. During this time, they purchased a farm off Austin Springs Road that became known as "The Mile Long Farm."

Finley Alison House

Finley Alison (1774-1833) was the brother of Robert and the youngest son of John Alison Sr. He arrived with the rest of his family in 1779 from Maryland. Finley married Susannah King (1799-1831), daughter of William and Elizabeth Sharp King whom emigrated to the area about 1780.

Finely and Susannah built their home between 1811-1813 on land which he inherited from his father. This well-preserved and well cared for hand fired brick antique home is listed on the National Register of Historic Places. The brick walls in the home are 18 inches thick with a 29-inch thick limestone foundation forming the ground floor walls. The woodwork of the staircase and five mantels show outstanding architectural quality. The high ceilings and ornamental plaster demonstrates the excellent taste of the builder.

In 1882, ownership of the house came back into the Alison Family after many years with other owners. Today, descendants of the Alison family owns the house.

(Photo By: Rene Rutherford)
Built between 1811-1813, The Finley Alison House is on the National Register of Historic Places.

Finley and Susannah had one daughter whom they named Susannah. She married W.B. Long and they also had one daughter and named her Susannah Logan. Susannah Logan married William Smith and they had one son, William N. Smith.

The Finley Alison family had several tragedies happen unfortunately. First, at the age of 32 Finley's wife, Susannah died in 1831. Next, in 1833 on a Sunday morning while the rest of the Alison Family went to church at New Bethel Finley stayed behind. When the family returned from the service. They saw Finley lying on the ground at the base of the long steep staircase leading to the veranda of his home. When the family approached him, he was dead. Apparently of a broken neck suffered from. the fall down his staircase. Finally, Finley and Susannah's daughter, Susanah Long, died at the tender age of 18.

Jesse Alison House

Jesse Alison was the son of Captain "Jack" John Alison Jr. and Martha Hodge Alison. After Captain Jack Alison's death in 1832, Jesse purchased the divided interests from the seven living heirs "to the 428 acre John Alison Sr. home tract." Jesse then became the sole owner of the old John Alison home place and the great virgin hardwood forest. The virgin forest on his property was one of the largest expanses of virgin forest east of the Mississippi River. About forty years ago, it was logged for its timber. Jesse lived in the home place until it burned. Jesse built the large three-story mansion in 1856 across the road from the original John Alison Sr. homestead. Andrew Shell, one of the contractors hired to build this great house, purchased iron lining for the fireplaces from an iron furnace in Stoney Creek. The bricks for the building were burned in a kiln near a spring. The spring water was piped to the house in lead pipes. The house was three full stories high plus a cellar and an attic. The bricks were laid three to four bricks thick on the exterior walls and interior main petitions. Porches extended out from each floor of the house with large doors opening to the porches. Two hand fired brick chimneys flanked the house.

In its time, the Jesse Alison House was an architectural specimen. Like the Finley Alison House, the Jesse Alison House is on the National Register of Historic Places. However, it is unfortunate that through years of neglect and vandalism, the mansion is now a pile of bricks. As a child I remember riding through the Alison Forest and am struck with fear as we approached this intimidating house. Even in its dilapidated state that I remember it, there was still a sense of awe as you imagined how beautiful in once was.

During the Civil War, two mounted men dressed as soldiers came to the house and arrested Jesse. These men were later proven to be common "bushwhackers" and Jesse was released.

Jesse's son Carlie lived in the house his entire life. People in Piney Flats refer to the remains as the Carlie Alison Mansion.

Torbett House

Along with the Alison's, Massengill's, and King's the Torbett family were among the early settlers in the Fork Country of Piney Flats.

John Torbett and Alexander Torbett Sr. paid taxes on land in Sullivan County in 1796. Alexander's taxable land totaled 100-acres which he sold to John in 1797. The home was built between 1797-1798, and inherited by John's son Hugh who was born in the house about 1818. Hugh and his wife Elizabeth raised seven children in this house.

The house was built of hewn logs that were visible during restoration work that was done on the house by its current owners. Where the chimney once stood you could see a portion of the original structure built by John Torbett. Today the descendants of John Torbett still live in the area and continue to serve the community well.

(Photo By: Rene Rutherford)
The Oliver Mansion, built c.1855, is one of the finest homes in Piney Flats, yet it's builder is a mystery.

Oliver Mansion

There is a mystery about the builder of the Oliver Mansion. It is believed that John Oliver was the builder of this beautiful house however; in 1855 Mr. Oliver paid $2721 for the place. Either he paid a lot for the land or he paid for the land with the house already built. Nevertheless, the Oliver Mansion is a delightful home.

John Oliver purchased the land from the heirs of Mary McCorkle Scott, wife of Colonel John Scott. Colonel Scott served as Justice of the Peace and Sheriff of Sullivan County. He was Lieutenant Colonel of the Sullivan County militia, and one of the first Representatives from this county to serve in the North Carolina Legislature.

This beautiful two-story hand fired brick mansion has two great brick chimneys, and four fireplaces with walnut mantels. The walls are plastered and the fine staircase goes to the second floor central hall. The house has the original hardware and all the doors and windows are pegged. The six over six paned windows remain on all four sides of this lovely home. Two small attic windows flank the chimneys on each end of the house.

By 1868, John Oliver had moved to Washington County North Carolina and the house was then occupied by Uriah C. Oliver. In 1907 Uriah and his wife A.J., transferred the property title to James R. Hughes of California, but reserved the rights for Uriah and his wife to "live out their natural lives here," and "have right to dwell in and control the house and the kitchen and smokehouse, the spring and springhouse, the tenant house, the blacksmith shop, the granary, the corn crib, and so much of the barn as they need, also the orchard and fruit and to have reasonable number of hogs, cows, and horses, a number of trucks and to have one sixth of the products of the farm for their support."

I think they covered every detail.

Sources:
Holston Territory Genealogical Society. *Families and History of Sullivan County, Tennessee Volume One 1779-1792*. Waynesville, NC: Walsworth Publishing, 1992.

Spoden, Murial C. *Historic Sites of Sullivan County*. Kingsport, TN: Kingsport Press, 1976.

Chapter
Four

New Bethel, The Union Church, and Mary Hughes

Two factors contribute to the development of a community. They are the church and the schools. Piney Flats is no different when it comes to these factors. The church provides a meeting place for the members of the community and gives its congregation an identity. It allows other members of the church to have a special bond with each other. In small communities, your church is a matter of pride. Every church in the community wants to be considered the best. Therefore, when a member of another church or a complete stranger visits your congregation they are sure that the utmost of hospitality will be shown. In the event of a member of another church in the community becoming unhappy with its current congregation and they begin attending another church in the community, they are made to feel as if they had attended the church their entire life. Piney Flats does have the uniqueness of having a wide variety of churches to choose from. All interestingly enough get along very well with each other. Another uniqueness in a small community.

The second factor that brings a community together is its school. Now before 1897 there was no official school in Piney Flats. There were schools established at the churches scattered throughout the community. These "Church Schools" continued to serve as schools after the development of a community wide school. However, after the formation of an expanded building and accredited four-year high school, these small "Church Schools" began to slowly die out. This marked an end of an era to some but the birth of unity and pride for an entire community. In small communities, the local high school becomes the central focal point for most of the citizens. The "community school" represents not only a community but each individual as well. When your school is playing in the big game against your archrival, usually the next community or town, everything shuts down and all eyes are focused on the game. Cheering loudly and supporting the team any way you can, you rejoice with joy when your team wins giving you bragging rights until the teams play again.

Schools and churches provide a community with much of its entertainment. Plays, cantatas, musicals, dances (at schools), fairs, and pageants would fill the calendars of most of the citizens. Bring all faiths and lifestyles together in one comfortable setting.

During this section we will focus on these two factors and understand why their development strengthens the already tight knit community of Piney Flats.

Mary Hughes School

The first school in the community of old Piney Flats was held in the former slave cabins on Samuel Hughes' farm, about a half- mile from the present day school of Mary Hughes. Schools in the outlying areas of the community that preceded this school on the Hughes farm were located in various churches such as New Bethel (1782), Locust Grove (now Edgefield-1847), Rocky Springs (1844), Poplar Ridge (1850). Deerlick (1883), and Mountain View (c.1886). The first school was described in 1868 as having one room with a colonial fireplace and a large chimney. The students sat on long benches without backs.

Classes were held in this former slave cabin of Hughes until 1873 when Shell's Chapel Union Church was erected and classes were moved to the church. Former students of the school remember it being weatherboard on the outside and on the inside was one room with two rows of benches. The school at Shell's Chapel educated the citizens of Piney Flats for 24 years.

In late 1896, citizens of the community elected a board of trustees for the purpose of erecting a community school. Samuel Dale Hughes gave a title bond to one and a half acres of land for a school site. He placed the following five restrictions on the deed: the building was to be completed within two years; it was to be at least 40 feet wide and 60 feet long; it was to be a brick structure two stories high; the sale of intoxicating beverages was prohibited; and the local Masonic order was to have one room for meetings. Citizens of the community immediately began work on the burning of brick for the building.

During the construction of the school, many citizens of the community did most of the work. S.M. Warren, J.N. Arrants, A.M. Shell, and W.R. Shell were members of the community that were recognized as contributing greatly to the project. The workers' hours were from sun-up to sun-down with a two-tier pay scale- ($.25 for boys and $.5O for men for a days work. A kiln was constructed on the site of the present-day auditorium for the burning of bricks. It was during the operation of this kiln in the spring of 1897 that Samuel Hughes contracted pneumonia, which led to his death before the school was completed. Nora Wolfe, Betty Arrants, Lula Hughes, and Lelia Patterson, heirs of Samuel Hughes made the deed for the property on which the school was located, on August 30, 1897.

(Photo By: Rene Rutherford)
Mary Hughes, the pride of Piney Flats, has educated thousands of children during it's one-hundred plus years of existence.

In September of 1897 less than one year after construction began, the first students entered the new four-room structure. The trustees selected Mary Hughes Institute as the name of the new school in memory of Samuel Hughes' wife. W.R. Page was the first principal of Mary Hughes Institute and J.E.L. Seneker was the current superintendent of schools. Although there was some county support and supervision in its early days, Mary Hughes Institute had many characteristics of a private school. Tuition of $1 a month was charged f or grades 1-4, $1.25 a month for grades 5-6, and $2 for special classes. Subjects taught included algebra, plane geometry, rhetoric, civil government, philosophy, trigonometry, solid geometry, Latin, piano, voice, and education.

Mrs. Lelia Hughes Taylor attended school at the first Mary Hughes. She described the school as an extraordinary building with large rooms and huge windows that let in brilliant rays of sunlight. She complimented the teachers of her youth, especially Myrtle Sanders. Mrs. Taylor remembered how beautiful Ms. Sanders was and how she would buy or make gifts for her students which she paid for out of her own pocket. In those days teachers were paid very little and were only provided with the three B's: a Broom, a Bucket, and a Box of chalk, forcing them to be very creative.

Children in those early days were no different than those today. According to Mrs. Taylor, pranks and flirting were practiced daily as well as being strong willed. If a boy took interest in you he would walk by your desk and drop chinquapins on your desk. These would be tied together to make a necklace for the lucky girl. The boys were not allowed to set near the girls so they had to be sly when pursuing a possible girlfriend.

A favorite practical joke would be to dip the braids of a girl that sat in front of you in the ink well that was on your desk. When the unfortunate victim stood up, ink would be scattered all over her and those within a close proximity.

Mrs. Taylor gives her class the recognition as organizing the first set down strike in America. When they completed their elementary studies, and were to be promoted to the "big room with the man teacher in it," they refused to go and protested by setting down in their old room. The mutiny was quickly subdued when the teachers threatened to tell their older brothers and sisters about their action. They knew that their parents would find out if big brother or big sister were told.

Before 1920, students who had completed a course of study at Mary Hughes Institute took a college entrance exam before continuing their education. In the fall of 1920, the Institute became a three- year high school. Students finished their education by enrolling in accredited four-year high schools in neighboring towns. In the fall of 1923, Mary Hughes Institute became an accredited four-year high school. At this time the faculty consisted of three teachers and the course of study included mathematics, English history, teacher training, and domestic sciences. J. Craft Akard Sr. was the superintendent of schools. The first senior class graduated in commencement exercises held in the Union Church in the spring of 1924. The class of 24 had five graduates: M.D. Massengill, J.B. Warren, Paul Shell, Opal Shell, and Margie Lynn Allison. Those students that had the privilege of attending Mary Hughes during its infancy respected their teachers and were very disciplined.

It was believed that if you did not paddle a student you were not doing your job. These strict standards made Mary Hughes a well-respected institution.

The 20's were a time of growth and expansion for Mary Hughes Institute. Not only did it become a four year accredited high school and graduate its first class, but also it added classes and expanded it's building and added other programs and services. In 1924, four classrooms and an auditorium were added. In 1925 a vocational agriculture program was added thanks to the Smith- Hughes Act of 1917 that provided the funds for the program. In 1929, citizens of the community, with some county support, built one of the first Gymnasiums in East Tennessee. (The Gym was located on the present day site of the outdoor basketball courts at the school) In 1921, the first PTA of the school was organized with Mrs. R.S. Shell as the first president. Their first project was to provide three large stone fountains with a spigot at the bottom to replace the zinc buckets with a dipper in use at the time. The next major project was to purchase a piano for the school. Funds were raised by the raffle of two quilts made by PTA members. In the late 20's, the PTA bought equipment for the Home Economics classroom that had just been organized. In 1928, the group paid half of the cost of digging a well to replace the cistern. The county agreed to pay the other half of the total cost of $1200. It took the PTA over one year to raise their half.

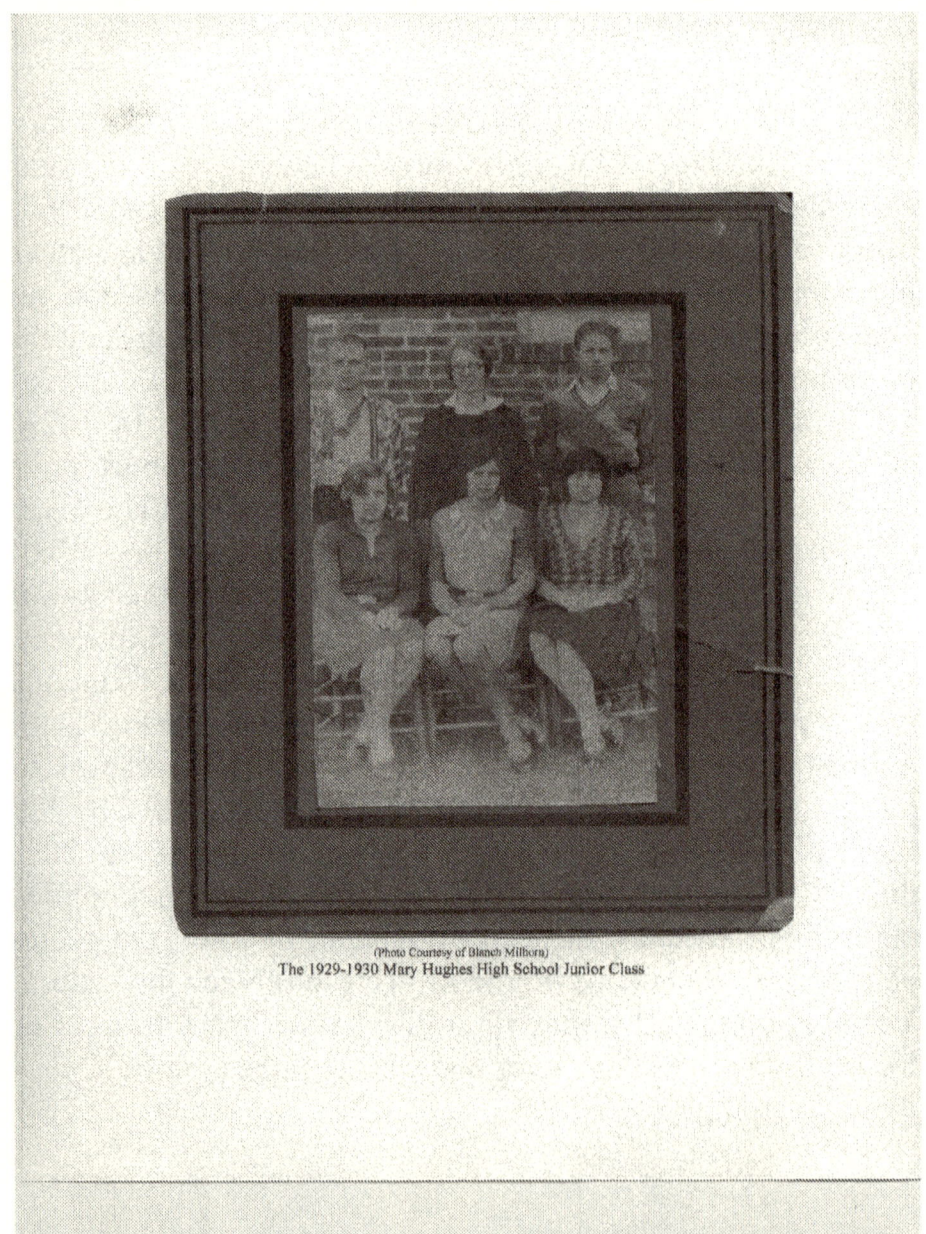

(Photo Courtesy of Blanch Milhora)
The 1929-1930 Mary Hughes High School Junior Class

The community life of Piney Flats was enriched by the activities of the school and its faculty. For a number of years teachers boarded in the homes of the community, further increasing their influence on the students. Several early faculty members were considered outstanding in their field of study. Gertrude Sanders Ford was known for her methods of teaching elementary reading. She conducted training and demonstrations at the Teacher Normal School (now East Tennessee State University) in 1916. Other outstanding teachers Mary Hughes Institute were Mae Akard, Lola Pyle, O.L. Jones, and the Sanders sisters-Maude, Gertrude, and Mytrle.

By the 1930's, the property on which the school was located had been deeded to the county, allowing the board of education to fully finance an addition. These additions consisted of a combination study hall-library with an office and storage space. An athletic program was underway which produced some of the most outstanding football and girl's basketball teams of the decade in East Tennessee. Coach Steve Lacy started the football program at Mary Hughes. Milligan College provided the equipment for the team. The football team recorded victories over Bristol Tennessee High, Blountville, Jonesborough, Happy Valley, and Moshiem. All were very respected programs in East Tennessee. The boy's basketball and baseball teams also had very successful season during the 1930's at Mary Hughes. In 1934, under the direction of Miss Gladys Carr, the Mary Hughes Lady Lions girl's basketball team won the regional championship. The 1930's were without a doubt a very successful time for Mary Hughes athletics. However, with the coming of WW II athletics would take a back seat to more important issues.

In 1936, the state board of education ruled that each accredited high school must have an adequate library. At that time the entire high school library was contained in a single bookcase, the contents of which was one set of encyclopedias, a few reference books, and some works of fiction. The PTA began a project to correct this deficiency, and by the early part of 1941, they had placed five hundred dollars' worth of new books in the library- just before the building burned.

(Photo courtesy of Blanch Milhorn)
The 1929-1930 Mary Hughes Girls Basketball Team.

On April 11, 1941, Mary Hughes School burned. Only the gym was left intact. Work began at once on a new building. Alley Construction of Bristol built the new building at a cost of $108,128.00. When completed, the new school had 14 large classrooms, 3 smaller classrooms, an office, an auditorium, and shop facilities. During the 1941-1942 school year, high school classes were held in the gymnasium, while elementary classes met in a storage building belonging to Wolfe Brothers Furniture Company. The 1942-1943 school year began with all classes in the new building.

Increased enrollment created an urgent demand for additional space. In 1949 a new gym, cafeteria, and Masonic Hall were added. In 1953, more space was needed and an addition of six new classrooms and a library with office space was added. Tragedy struck again in November 1956, when the 1953 addition burned. Only a combination of luck, timing, wind, and help from the community saved the remainder of the school. Classes in the burned-out area met in the Piney Flats Union Church for the remainder of the school year. Rebuilding was completed by the 1957-1958 school year.

Mary Hughes High School came to an end in 1968. Sullivan County Board of Education agreed to consolidate their high schools. Mary Hughes, Bluff City, and Holston Valley combined to form Sullivan East High School for the 1968-1969 school year. Debates over the issue of consolidation became very heated. Many did not favor the idea of a large high school. They felt a smaller environment would be more conducive to learning. County Magistrate Ed Alison argued against the issue while Superintendent J.C. Akard argued for consolidation. While they were debating in front of the county commission Mr. Alison suffered a major heart attack and died fighting for what he believed in. Nevertheless, the commission decided that it would cost the county too much money to make improvements on the smaller schools needed to bring them to state standards.

Mary Hughes continued as an elementary and junior high school. In 1977, the middle school system was adopted in Sullivan Count making Mary Hughes a K-8 middle school.

Continued population growth gave Mary Hughes School an enrollment over 500 students, more than when it was a 1-12 high school. By the 1980's time and stiffer fire and safety, codes made necessary extensive repairs to the aging school. In the spring and summer of 1986 major work on the building resulted in the removal of asbestos, a new lighting system, a fire alarm and fire door system, lowered ceilings, new paint for most of the school, a new kindergarten complex, and rebuilding of the former shop area to house art, music, and band class. In 1998, the gymnasium was named in honor of former principal and head basketball coach, Dwight Mason. Under Coach Mason's tutelage, Mary Hughes won two Upper Lakes Conference championships.

(Photo courtesy of Blanch Milhorn)
The 1934-1935 Mary Hughes Boys Basketball Team.

Today Mary Hughes serves as the only K-8 school in Sullivan County. Over the last one hundred years Piney Flats has closed the doors of eight schools located throughout the community and sent their students to Mary Hughes. As times have changed so to has Mary Hughes School, making it compatible to the fast paced world in which we live today. Mary Hughes has educated its students to the finest degree and better preparing them to be able and productive citizens.

Unfortunately, due to recent budget crunches the idea of making Mary Hughes only an elementary school and closing the middle school has been up for discussion. When this information reached the public, scores of parents and residents of Piney Flats unified to make their opinions known that they need Mary Hughes. One rumor that circulated throughout the community during this time was about the mother of Superintendent Dr. John O'Dell (a 1966 graduate of Mary Hughes). It was said that she locked him out of her house and would not let him in because of the proposal to close part of Mary Hughes. Shortly after, the proposal was dropped. Was it because of Dr. Odell's mother? We will never know. What we do know is Mary Hughes remains as an elementary and middle school.

However, the situation is very delicate and any year could be the last

for this great school. As long as the doors of Mary Hughes School are open, it will continue its mission to educate the children and prepare them for the world that eagerly awaits their contributions.

Sources:
Mary Hughes Homecoming '86,
Lelia Hughes Taylor Interview, 1987,
Nell Starnes, *Mary Hughes Parent Teacher Association. 1953.*

A Brief History of New Bethel

New Bethel Presbyterian Church has a treasured history that dates back to the Revolutionary era. New Bethel ranks as one of the oldest churches in Tennessee.

The Rev. Dr. Joseph Rhea laid the foundation for the congregation after visiting the area in the 1770's. Rev. Rhea was chaplain of a military campaign to restore the peace between Indians and the settlers of the area. While on assignment, Rev. Rhea fell in love with the area and decided to make this his new home. When he returned to his home in Maryland, he convinced his family and many members of his Piney Creek Church to move with him to present day Sullivan County. From 1777 to 1778, many families made the move from their homes in Maryland. However, Rev. Rhea never got to live in the land he loved, he died before he made the trip. The settlers became a congregation anyway, without a pastor or a house of worship. Their congregation became known as the "Church of the Forks," named so because of its proximity to the Holston and Watauga Rivers

In April of 1777, the Reverend Charles Cummings visited the area for a brief period and urged the congregation to build a house of worship. The building was completed in 1777 and became known as the Massengill House of Worship. Unfortunately during a Tory revolt in 1779 the building was destroyed.

The Reverend Samuel Doak was assigned by the General Assembly of the Presbytery to serve an area from

Ingles Ferry on the New River in Virginia to Dandridge in present day East Tennessee for "Home Missions." Rev. Doak is regarded as Tennessee's first minister. Unlike ministers before him, Doak made his home in Tennessee. During his time, Doak established 25 churches.

Doak completed the work started by Rhea when, under his leadership, the Presbytery officially organized the Church of the Forks in 1782. At that time, Doak renamed the church New Bethel after the Bethel Church in Stanton, Virginia where he had first preached.

Samuel Doak's preaching was described as "original, bold, pungent, and sometimes pathetic. His delivery was natural and impressive, and will fitted to give effect to the truths which he uttered." Reverend Doak is the preacher that stood before the gathering of frontier warriors at Sycamore Shoals. It was there that he prayed and blessed those that would turn the tide of the American Revolution at the Battle of Kings Mountain (October 7, 1780). His benediction over them was "The Sword of the LORD and of Gideon."

(Photo By: Andy Hare)
New Bethel Presbyterian Church established in 1782.

(Photo By: Rene Rutherford)
The New Bethel Cemetery began in 1790 when an unknown traveler was found dead on the Church grounds.

In 1782, New Bethel still sat in the middle of the frontier. The Cherokee Indians still considered this land as part of their ancient hunting grounds. There were two incident between Rev. Doak and the Cherokees. Reverend Doak was away in Abington getting supplies; Indians attacked his cabin and burned his house forcing Mrs. Doak to flee with their child. She fled to Rocky Mount for safety with her baby in her arms not making a sound.

In yet another encounter with the Indians, Reverend Doak was in mid-sermon when he saw a group of Indians coming toward the church. He paused, gave the benediction and joined the rescue party. These events may or may not have happened while he was at New Bethel, but nevertheless they give a great testimony to the danger of living in the frontier.

Doak placed a high priority on education. A school was also organized and James Gregg Sr., one of the elders of the session, served as the first teacher in the first school of Sullivan County.

This first building that served New Bethel was made of logs, had a shingled roof, and a stone chimney at the east end. The pulpit was in the west end, around which the male portion of the church gathered. The women and children occupied the end near the chimney.

Increase in the church membership in 1838, required an addition which was erected of hewn logs and joined to the west end. The pulpit was then in the middle of the north side of the church.

Log cabins served the congregation until 1873 when the present sanctuary was built. The bricks were made on site and the bell was shipped from Philadelphia.

New Bethel Presbyterian Church has been serving Sullivan County as a house of worship for well over two hundred years.

Among its former members buried in its cemetery are veterans of the American Revolution, War of 1812, Mexican-American War, the Civil War (Confederate and Union soldiers), Spanish-American War, World War I, and World War II. New Bethel's Cemetery offers us a glimpse into our hallowed past and allows people a chance to pay tribute to those who paved the way for our lives today.

The New Bethel Cemetery was formed in 1790 by a strange occurrence. An unknown traveler had fallen from his horse and died at the church. When the stranger was discovered no one knew who he was. However, his horse was still at his side and in the saddlebag was a small stone with the letters "I.G." inscribed on it. His body was buried at the church and the stone became the grave marker. The grave and the stone are there to this day. In the early days of the cemetery, the men that lived near the church prepared the graves. When the church bell rung three times the men would drop what they were doing and go to the cemetery to dig the grave.

For over two hundred and twenty years the congregation at New Bethel has served this area, more than fifty years longer than any other church in Piney Flats. There have been many changes and exciting events in this country and New Bethel Presbyterian Church has been there to see them all. In an era when change and being different is hip, New Bethel stays as it has been since 1782. As a matter of fact, the ruling Elders at New Bethel is the oldest continual governing body in the state of Tennessee. Proving that change is not always a good thing.

Source:
New Bethel Presbyterian Church. *The New Bethel Bicentennial 1782-1982*. Johnson City, TN: Overmountain Press, 1996.

The Union Church

The story of the Union Church in Piney Flats demonstrates the togetherness this community once had. Just imagine four different denominations worshipping in the same building. It is hard for us to comprehend this concept in today's time. The thought of a Union Church would not even be tolerated. For those that attended the Union Church were happy to have a building to worship in.

The history of the Piney Flats Union Church began when Andrew Shell gave land for the building of a union church. Shell who had help establish other churches in the area once served as a rider on the Methodist circuit of ministers. By the time Shell's Chapel had been established, he had retired from the circuit yet still acted as a major spiritual leader in the church.

The church was located on a knoll of pines just to the East of the present day site of Wolfe Brothers Furniture Factory. It was a white-framed weatherboard structure with a small belfry. At most churches of the nineteenth century, there were two sets of doors, one for the men and one for the women. At Shell's Chapel, however, there was one wide double door at the entrance. These were installed for the convenience of pall- bearers moving coffins in and out of the church for funerals.

Inside the building were two rows of pews, roughly twelve pews on each side, and two benches on the right hand corner that became known as "Amen Corner." These seats were for the select few gentlemen that wanted to respond to the sermon with a fervent "Amen" or "Yes LORD!"

Why was this church called a "union church?" Unlike many other churches in the area, Shell's Chapel housed four denominations of the protestant faith: Methodist (Methodist Episcopal, and Methodist Episcopal South), Presbyterians, and Baptist. Each denomination would be granted a designated Sunday every month. If your denomination was not going to deliver the sermon until the next week, you still went to church to hear the sermon of a different denomination anyway.

The minutes from some of the early days have survived and give us a wonderful look at the past. Mr. Edward W. Hughes made this interesting entry on June 7, 1879, "...forty-eight teachers and scholars were present, plus visitors and deadbeats..., for not everyone went inside; a few always remained outdoors in the shade of the pines to tell tales, swap knives, and referee dog fights." My, how times have changed!

(Photo By: Jennette Howze)
The Piney Flats United Methodist Church once served as a house of worship for four denominations of
Christians from the late 1870's to the 1950's.

Shell's Chapel remained in service until 1913 when a larger building was needed to fit the growing congregation. By this time Piney Flats was a busy village with industry, electricity, and telephone service.

The new location for the church would be next to Shell's Cemetery. At first the new church was to only house the Methodist Episcopal South followers. But due to the persistence of Cordelia Naff Shell, who owned the land in which the new building was to be built, the church retained its union church status. She was quoted saying; "I want a union church, or I don't want a church at all."

On January 10, 1915 the Piney Flats Union Church was finally completed. The new church was solid brick with stained glass windows. The floor was slopped downward so the congregation in the back could get a good view of the preacher. The church today, now the Piney Flats United Methodist Church, has only changed slightly. The same stained glass windows remain as well as the unique slope of the floor, though not as great of a slope. The sanctuary has been enlarged but for the most part the old Union Church looks similar today as it did in 1915.

How did four denominations meet in the same building? The Methodist Episcopal South had the first Sunday of the month, Presbyterians the second week, Methodist Episcopal the third week, and Baptist the fourth week. In the months with five Sundays, no regular schedule was set. Usually, a traveling preacher conducted services on these fifth Sundays. On the other scheduled services, the pulpit was supplied by circuit riders that came on horseback, in buggies, or by train and stayed with a member of the congregation.

Aside from the uniqueness of having four denominations in the same church, equally interesting is why there were two Methodist denominations. R.N. Price wrote in Volume III of his book *Holston Methodism* that the Methodist Church split over the issue of bishops in the church owning slaves. In 1844, the Methodist Church split into the Northern branch and the Southern branch. By 1939, this issue in Piney Flats had become somewhat redundant. Consequentially, leaders from each branch agreed to organize as one denomination; forming the Piney Flats United Methodist

Church. This merger did not affect the Union Church. The only change was now the Methodist Church met on two Sundays a month.

By the 1950's, the Baptist membership in the Union Church had been reduced to only one family and regular services were stopped. However, the Methodist and Presbyterian congregations were flourishing. After a study group met to discuss the future of the Union Church, it was decided that it was in the best interest to have two separate churches.

(Photo By: Rene Rutherford)
Shell's Cemetery has served as the final resting place for many residents of Piney Flats including Andrew Shell for whom the cemetery is named.

In the late Fall of 1958, the Methodist Church bought out the Presbyterian interest in the union Church thus giving the Methodist sole possession of the church building. By that next spring, the Presbyterians had built their new church and the Union Church was no more.

Even though the Union Church ceased to exist after 1958, its legacy continues to this day. The Piney Flats United Methodist Church, Piney Flats Presbyterian Church, and the Piney Flats Baptist Church all gained their origins out of this unified church.

In a way, when the Union Church dissolved, Piney Flats lost some of its identity. It seems now looking back on our history, this is the first domino to fall in the decline of a unified and recognized community. That same year the train depot was torn down and ten years later in 1968 Mary Hughes graduated its last senior class. Then Highway 11E was widened and most of the communities industry moved closer to the more convenient four-lane. Finally the annexation battles over the last twenty years among three cities have all but taken away what Piney Flats once was.

Source:
Piney Flats United Methodist Church. *History of Piney Flats United Methodist Church*. 1983.

Andrew Shell

It is impossible to do research on Piney Flats without finding the name Andrew Shell mentioned. His contributions to the development of this community are immeasurable. Words do not give enough credit to Andrew Shell for his greatness. I felt that it is only necessary to tell who Mr. Shell was.

Andrew Shell was born in 1797 on the banks of the Holston River four miles north of Bluff City. He married Winnifred Boy, also from the Holston River area, in his early manhood. After they were married, they moved to Indiana but returned back to Tennessee after several years. Upon their arrival back home they acquired land in present day Piney Flats, where they settled and lived the rest of their days.

It is Andrew Shell that the early village of Piney Flats was first named. Before the building of the train depot in 1858, the area in which they settled was given the name, "Shell's Crossings" or sometimes "Shell's Cross-roads." Shell contributed greatly to the development of Piney Flats as a whole. He was one of the first settlers, he was the first Post Master, and gave the land for the first church in Piney Flats.

In addition to his many jobs in Piney Flats, he was also a contractor. In 1856, Jesse Alison hired Shell to build his massive Alison Mansion. The Mansion, now demolished due to severe vandalism, was on the National Register of Historic Places.

91

Shell was given the name "Father Shell," by many of the residents of Piney Flats because of his influence in the development of the community and his background as a Methodist clergyman. Shell served as a rider on the Methodist circuit in the area. Shell helped establish the church at Locust Grove. This church later became Edgefield United Methodist Church and still serves the area today. In addition to the church at Locust Grove, Shell also contributed greatly to the development of the Bluff City Methodist Church.

In 1873, Shell donated one of his three thousand acres for the building of a union church in Piney Flats. This church was given the name Shell's Chapel in his honor. Even though retired from the Methodist rider circuit, he remained active as a spiritual leader in the community.

Andrew Shell answered to many names; Dr. Shell, Reverend Shell, Father Shell, or Mr. Shell but whatever he was called it was spoke with the utmost respect. He was one of Piney Flats first and most beloved residents. The cemetery at the Piney Flats United Methodist Church still bears the name "Shell's Cemetery" in his honor. It is here that Andrew Shell was laid to rest on April 11, 1880, after ninety years of serving the LORD and his community.

Source:
Piney Flats United Methodist Church. *History of Piney Flats United Methodist Church.* 1983.

Chapter
Five

Memories from the Past

In this next segment I will take you on a journey through the past and introduce you to some of the memories that helped make Piney Flats stand out from other communities. From the formation of the lighted croquet court to the Sullivan County Fair, Piney Flats developed its identity. These brief excerpts give us the pleasure of seeing the dedication of the men and women of Piney Flats that made this community source of great pride.

Some of these stories are from the distant past while others are from my memory. Sit back and enjoy the past being brought to the present. If you look closely you may remember these great events and activities of our past.

Croquet Anyone?

During the 1950's in Piney Flats, people would gather in the area around the train depot and general stores in the evenings. The purpose; to "loaf." Loafing is an art form that many men in Piney Flats had perfected. I remember as a young man my friends and me would find places to loaf during the summer evenings. We felt that if we were to be complete citizens in Piney Flats we had to learn this art form.

The ability to loaf is a process that takes years to learn. First, you need people, at least four or five. Second, you need a place to meet. Usually a central location that is easy to get to. This location needs to be in an area that is relatively visible to the public so they can see who the best loafers are in the community. Third, you need to learn how to brag on yourself about your work ethic. It is imperative that a good loafer can tell every detail of the day's work you just completed. (Seasoned loafers know the advanced art of exaggeration when telling a story) Finally, you need something to occupy your time. An activity that is enjoyed by all but requires little effort.

It was during one of these loafing evenings that the leading loafers in the community began churning up ideas of activities that might occupy their time. One of the loafers suggested the game of croquet. Croquet was a game that was not common to many but it was enjoyable and low intensity. After the matter was discussed, it was decided that a croquet court be built in Piney Flats. Construction began immediately. The first two courts were very able courts, however they were not official courts. These were made on grass and a real croquet court is built on a hard packed sand-like surface. Finally building was completed behind the depot in the early 1950's of an authentic croquet course.

Every night the gentlemen loafers of Piney Flats would play croquet and the talent became very competitive. As word spread throughout the surrounding areas other loafers from other communities began competing against the Piney loafers. It became so popular that lights were added to the course so the games could go on at night. This court was undoubtedly the only one of its kind in Sullivan County and some sources have said that it was the only lighted croquet court in the South.

By the late 60's, the fad of playing croquet in Piney Flats had died out. Nevertheless for a short period of time, next to Mary Hughes basketball, croquet was king in Piney Flats.

The County Fair

County fairs are a very festive time. They bring out the kid in all of us. They are an opportunity to show of some your special talents, to impress, to compete, to be entertained, and to fellowship. These fairs may be the only time in a year that you may see old friends. It is a time to see new and innovative advancements in technology. Fairs have been part of our country's history for years and Piney Flats did not miss out on the opportunity to host several of these events.

Early in the 1900's Piney Flats started the Sullivan County Fair at Locust Grove (Edgefield Church). This became an extremely popular event throughout the region. In 1932 the fair relocated to Mary Hughes School. At one fair over 6,000 people attended! There were contests ranging from needlework to livestock competitions. Mary Hughes School served as exhibition halls with displays set throughout the building. There was also a wide variety of entertainment. Balloon flights, parachute jumps, carnivals, foot races, baseball games, baby shows, beauty contests, largest foot contests and no fair would be complete without the pie-eating contest.

Sadly, the fair had grown to big for Piney Flats and had to move to Blountville in the late 1930's. Blountville could accommodate the vast number of people that were attending this festive event. However, the fair did not last long in Blountville and was discontinued. Nevertheless, for thirty years Piney Flats brought the people of Sullivan County together for celebration and festivities.

Source:
Anderson, John. "Historical Dates and Items of Interest on Mary Hughes School, and Town, and Community at Large." 1945.

Let There Be Light

The genius of the Wolfe family went well beyond their furniture and coffins or telephone company. They thought bigger. In fact they perceived Piney Flats as a village with a great deal of potential. So much potential that John Bunyan Wolfe decided to provide electricity to the community.

Originally, Wolfe, used a steam generator to provide power for his furniture factory. He then extended lines to his house and other stockholders in his company. As interest in this luxury grew, neighbors and friends requested lines to their homes. Wolfe agreed to their wishes and extended his services down Main Street and charged 1 dollar a month with the condition that their front porch light would be left on so the street would have some lighting.

Upon the marriage of John's son Samuel to Bess Wexler in 1912, the future of electricity in Piney Flats went from good to great. The former Miss Wexler's father gave his mill, the old Hyder Mill to the Wolfe family as a wedding present. This mill became the backbone of the source of power to everyone in Piney Flats. The Wolfe's decided to extend their service to everyone in Piney Flats by using the hydroelectric energy produced by the newly acquired mill.

The recipients of electricity were given one free outlet on their front porch that was not wired through the meter. This was to provide light for the streets. Homes far from Main Street, where well-lit streets were not necessary, were even given the free outlet. Naturally people would have as much as they could connect to this free outlet forcing a heavy drain on the generator. Several old timers of Piney Flats recall that you had to get up early in the morning to receive a strong electrical current into your home. As the day would wear on and more and more people turned their lights on, your light would get a little dimmer.

In 1941 the Piney Flats Electric Light Company was sold to the Johnson City Power Board. To many customers and to much strain on the generator forced the sell of the power plant. People were not allowed to keep their free front porch outlet anymore and now a stranger in another city would keep up with how much power they used. Yes it was an end to an era, but for about forty years Piney Flats had the distinction as the smallest village in the world with its own power plant.

Source: Muse, Betty. "Piney Flats Electric Light Company." *Families and Histories of Sullivan County, Tennessee Volume One 1779-1992.* Waynesville, NC: Walsworth Publishing, 1992.

John Bunyan Wolfe

Andrew Shell may have been the man that started Piney Flats, but it was Shell's grandson John Bunyan Wolfe that made it prosper. Born in 1857, Mr. Wolfe was a man of unusual vision. As a schoolboy, he and his sisters Addie, Effie, and Ellie worked with a lathe powered by a cane mill that the girls turned. Using the lathe and walnut fence rails, the children made posts and table legs.

With one hundred dollars earned from the sale of his horse, Wolfe bought an engine and set up his first furniture factory. Mr. Wolfe produced fine household furniture: cupboards, tables, bedroom suites, stools, cane-bottomed chairs, and coffins.

The business prospered and in 1906 his business was incorporated into Wolfe Brothers and Company. The Wolfe Brothers Furniture Factory stayed in operation until the 1980's.

Furniture and coffins were not the only items Wolfe made. In 1895 he built and partially owned the telephone system in Piney Flats with connections to Bristol and Elizabethton. The switchboard was operated in Mr. Wolfes home.

In 1918, Mr. Wolfe organized the Piney Flats Electric Light and Power Company. Powered by a dynamo at Hyders Mill on the Watauga River, residents of Piney Flats received electric light during certain hours of the day. Each home was given access to one free outlet on their front porch. As more and more people used the light during the

101

day, the lights would grow dimmer. The Power Company was sold to East Tennessee Light and Power Company of Johnson City in 1941.

Through Mr. Wolfe's genius, residents of Piney Flats enjoyed luxuries that not many rural communities had. His factory provided a good job for the men of the community, his telephone system allowed people to communicated with the outside world, and his power plant brought electric light into the homes of Piney Flats.

Muse, Betty. "Piney Flats Electric Light Company." *Families and Histories of Sullivan County, Tennessee Volume One 1779-1992.* Waynesville, NC: Walsworth Publishing, 1992.

Piney Flats Recreation Program

In the mid-1970's members of the Piney Flats Ruritan and area churches decided it would be nice to have a recreation program for the area children during the summers. The churches would donate money to the cause and the Ruritan would provide the building. Every summer for nearly twenty years children from 6-16 years of age would come to the Piney Flats Community Center from 12-4 P.M. for eight weeks.

Members of the local churches who would supervise the daily activities administered the program. Everyday snacks were served and an area minister would give a fifteen-minute devotion to the children. There were a wide variety of games to occupy the children's time. They had numerous board games, coloring books, Ping-Pong, croquet, billiards, air hockey, volleyball, yard darts, basketball, and the most popular; whiffleball. At the end of the program there would be a tournament in billiards (both eight ball and nine ball), Ping-Pong, air hockey, free throw shooting, and many more with an awards ceremony at the end.

The program averaged over seventy children a day and some days one hundred and thirty attended. It was a very positive influence on the youth of Piney Flats. Some of my fondest memories are of my time there. I still have my first place trophies from winning the billiards, Ping-Pong, and air hockey tournaments. I can also remember winning the unofficial whiffleball home run championship when I was twelve years old. It was such a great experience in not only my life but also everyone who ever attended this program. Six-year-olds would play with sixteen-year-olds, boys played with girls, and wealthy kids played with poor kids. No one cared who you were because you were there for the same reasons. Everyone just wanted to have fun. Even if there was a fight, and believe me there were many, you usually were friends before you left for the day. I consider myself very fortunate to have participated in this program.

Sadly, the program ceased in 1992. Churches quit sponsoring and no one would sacrifice the time to supervise anymore. I guess the emphasis churches place on youth groups might have been a cause. Churches began to place a strong emphasis on their own youth and progressively almost every church in Piney Flats hired a paid Youth Minister. The youth ministers would be responsible for their respective church having their own summer program. When the Piney Flats Recreation Program was established, volunteers led youth groups in churches. Now it is a different story.

Piney Flats Church Softball

On June 6, 1980, the Piney Flats Ruritan dedicated its new softball and community park to Edward (Ed) Cross. Mr. Cross donated the land to the Piney Flats Ruritan, for which he was a member, for the construction of the park. The park would stay in the Ruritan's name as long as the Piney Flats Ruritan would oversee it.

The park became an instant success in the community. From 1980-2000 the park would be the site of the Piney Flats Church Softball League. All the churches in Piney Flats and Bluff City competed in this popular league. The leagues purpose was to generate enthusiasm within the community and encourage fellowship among local churches. The Ruritan maintained the park itself and the churches paid for the umpires, softballs, and trophies. Men and women's league games were played on Monday, Tuesday, Thursday, and Friday from mid-May to early August.

The league became a very popular social event throughout the community and provided a good source of entertainment. It was not uncommon to have four or five hundred spectators enter the gates on a Friday night. The fans would come and socialize, eat some of the famous hamburgers from the concession stand and cheer on their church's team. The games at times were very competitive and sometimes you forgot you were at a church league game. The tournament champion at the end of the season would have bragging rights until the next season. Players on these championship teams became household names throughout the community. Even today you can still hear people talk about some of the early stars that played in the league.

Aside from the softball field and concession stand, the park also housed the Paty Pavillion for picnics and a playground for the children. I remember as a boy how I couldn't wait for the season to start. This gave me and the other children of the area a chance to have our own social events. We would play cup-ball, have foot races, go exploring in the fields, see who could build the best sand castles, flirt with girls, and every now and then have a fight or two. It is at this park that I felt real pain for the first time. I was five years old and decided that I was tough enough to pick a fight with a seven year old. Needless to say I did not do so well and my jaw still has a pop in it to this day from the episode.

Unfortunately, the churches decided to go elsewhere in 2001 thus ending a twenty-year tradition. The park is still open, and is now under the direction of Poplar Ridge Christian Church but you cannot hear the ping of the bat or the roar of the crowd. The sounds of playing children are also gone. All that remains is a lonely park full of beautiful memories.

The Talent Show

Probably some of the most enjoyable moments I had growing up were the "talent shows" we had at the Piney Flats Presbyterian Church. For over a dozen years members of the congregation would demonstrate their "talents" in methods that Jay Leno would have been proud of. These talents were usually spoofs of T.V. shows, songs, and music videos. It was a combination of the "Tonight Show" and "Saturday Night Live." It was our version of a variety show that displayed a wide range of so called talent.

The show was held in the fellowship hall of the church and usually last several hours, but it never felt that long. From the opening skit to the closing comments the audience would be in stitches from laughter. The show had something for all ages. Cute children's songs, imitations of old radio shows, and parities of popular T.V. shows and music personalities kept everyone entertained. When I was old enough to participate, I portrayed everything from Lassie to Jerry Lee Lewis. I loved every minute of it.

The creativity behind the popular "Talent Show" was the members of the church. Everyone able participated in some form. It really brought the church together. However, the mastermind and leading showman was Larry Torbett. He had such a talent for coming up with the best ideas. During the planning sessions, I would sit in amazement while he would organize and explain his ideas for the next show.

The "Talent Show" is a thing of the past. It has not been performed for several years. I hope one day it will be revived, but no matter what it will always live in my memories. I had the blessed pleasure to part of one of the most pleasant eras of Piney Flats Presbyterian Church. I will forever laugh at the remembrance of the "Talent Show" as I picture my family members on stage demonstrating their talents. I am thankful to the Church for giving me these fond memories of my family.

The Fall Festival

One event I could not wait to happen when I was growing up was the Mary Hughes Fall Festival. Every year the parents, faculty and staff, and clubs of Mary Hughes would put together an activity that would rival any festival in the area. It seemed to me that everybody in the community was there.

The classrooms were changed to exhibition halls and game rooms. The gym was packed with games and entertainment. Food stands were around every corner. Fire trucks and police cars were in the parking lot. There was even an auction of donations that local businesses gave. Best of all, the proceeds went back into the community. It was a real sight.

Words cannot explain the excitement I felt when the festival arrived. I thought the cakewalk was the greatest game around. It only cost a quarter and you had a chance to win nice big chocolate cake. I never won the cake, but the excitement was too much to withstand and I would beg my mom for another quarter.

Every kid in the school would gather all the stickers that were free. The best stickers were the ones the Armed Forces donated to give away. My notebooks would be full of Army, Navy, Air Force, and Marine stickers. Only the lucky ones were able to get one of the rare posters that were to be given away. My brother was the master at coming away with an *Aim High* U. S. Air Force poster.

It was at one of the Fall Festivals that I learned the value of honesty. I found a wad of money lying in the hallway. I thought it was my lucky day. My mom saw me with more money than she had and asked where I got it. I told her I found it in the hall. She encouraged me to turn it in to one of the festival administrators. It was one of the hardest things I had ever done in my short life. I thought whoever lost it did not want the money very badly since it was in the floor and I could sure use it to win that chocolate cake I coveted. Reluctantly, I turned the money in and as a reward they gave me a 3liter of Mountain Dew. I felt that I came out ahead since I had never seen a 3 liter of anything especially a 3 liter the super drink of every elementary students. I paraded around with my prize, the envy of all my classmates. I think I slept with that bottle that night.

The festival will always be a treasure in my memory. Even today when I see the Ruritan's sign at the crossroads promoting the upcoming festival, I get an extra burst of enthusiasm and I'm 9 years old again.

Chapter
Six

Sports Page

Like the rest of our country, sports have always been a major part in the everyday life of Piney Flats. I remember my first Major League baseball game that my parents took me to in New York City. I'll never forget walking into Yankee Stadium and setting in the right field stands as the Yanks defeated the Baltimore Orioles. Ever since I have a lifetime full of memories brought on by sports. My parents never forced sports upon me or my siblings but their background in sports influence me greatly. My mother, a '67 graduate of Mary Hughes High School, was a four-year varsity cheerleader and the 1967 Miss Mary Hughes winner. My father was an outstanding athlete from Pennsylvania. Out of high school the Boston Red Sox organization offered him a contract to be a pitcher in their farm league. His mother refused to sign for him and made him go to college. His college of choice was Arizona State, where he played for legendary coach Frank Kush. Dad suffered a career ending injury to his shoulder and forced him back to Pennsylvania. He later made his way to Milligan College where over the course of four years he lettered in basketball, baseball, and track and field. He went on to become a teacher and coach in Sullivan County for 32 years. While he served as head girl's basketball coach at Sullivan East, they won two conference championships in the mid-70's. As head track and field coach at East they won three county team championships and coached two individual state champions. My brother was one of only seven basketball players in the history of Sullivan East to play four years of college basketball. While in college he played at Northland Pioneer Junior College in Holbrook, Arizona two season and two seasons at Trevecca Nazerene University in Nashville. He scored over 1,200 points in college and was on the Academic All-American team. My sister was the 1986 Tennessee State high jump champion and runner-up in 1987. She dominated East Tennessee in track and field while attending Sullivan East. The *Kingsport Times News* sponsors the Times News Relay in which the winner of the most outstanding field events award for a female is the Krista Hare Outstanding Field Events Award. In college, she was a member of the M.T.S.U. track team, which won the 1988

Indoor Conference championship title and the 1990 Ohio Valley Athletic Conference high jump champion. I was a three-year All-Region player in baseball while at Sullivan East. I then played one season at E.T.S.U. and three seasons at Milligan College where I was a three-year team captain and All-Tennessee Virginia Athletic Conference member in 1998.

Piney Flats is full of similar stories of athletic success. Sports have given the residents of Piney Flats a source of opportunity for the players and entertainment for the spectators. Baseball was probably the first team sport played in Piney Flats because of the availability of open farmland. Farm boys would meet in a field and enjoy themselves in the therapeutic game that gave them an escape from the unending work they had to do day in and day out. Baseball tournaments would be held on the grounds at Mary Hughes during the early days of the Sullivan County fair.

Residents of Piney Flats have always been sports enthusiastic. Mary Hughes boasted one of the first gymnasiums in East Tennessee as well as arguably the finest clay tennis courts in the region. Both of these facilities were built in the late 1920's and early 1930's. Football became very popular in Piney Flats in the decade of the 30's. When the country was suffering from depression, people in Piney Flats escaped the troubles of the times by watching gridiron action or following the 1934-35 regional champion girls basketball team. In the 1950's and 1960's all of Piney Flats focused on the winter months to cheer on some the best high school basketball teams in the area. It must have been quite a sight to see the tiny gym at standing room only capacity. After consolidation residents of Piney Flats continue to this day its support of Mary Hughes as well as Sullivan East High Schools athletic teams.

Through the rich history of Piney Flats athletics I have decided to include whom I feel should be honored in an athletics hall of fame. I selected the following individuals based on one or a combination of the following criteria: their significant athletic accomplishments in high school, four years of participation in collegiate athletics, coaching contributions, or community involvement.

The 1934-1935 Mary Hughes Football and Girls Basketball Team.
(Photo Courtesy of Blanch Milhorn)

1934-1935 Mary Hughes Lady Lions Regional Champion Basketball Team

Frank McKenry

Frank Gordon McKenry, a.k.a. "Big Pete" or "Limb." Big Pete was born in Piney Flats on August 13, 1888 and went on to become the first and only resident of Piney Flats ever to play Major League baseball. From 1915 to 1916 McKenry pitched for the Cincinnati Reds of the National League. He compiled a career record of 6-6 with a 3.10 E.R.A. and 5 complete games. At the plate McKenry hit only .187, 7 hits in 38 at-bats, but pitchers are not supposed to hit. Mckenry died in Fresno California on November 11, 1956. Very few people in Piney Flats even know who McKenry was. I feel that it is finally time to recognize the "Piney Flats Rocket" Frank McKenry and give him the credit that is due for being the only Major Leaguer in the history of Piney Flats.

Jesse Milhorn

Jess, or J.D., played all sports at Mary Hughes High School in the early to mid 1930's. He was named as the right tackle on the all-time all-Mary Hughes football team. He played football at Milligan College for one season under the direction of coach Steve Lacy. He then transferred to E.T.S.U. where he pitched for legendary coach Dan Moody.

Claude Trivette

Claude Trivette, native of Piney Flats, was an outstanding high school athlete at Mary Hughes. He was listed as the running back on the all-time all-Mary Hughes football team. Football was not all he played. After high school he played and managed professionally in baseball during the late 30's and early 40's. In 1939 Trivette was an All-Star outfielder for the Kingsport Chiefs of the Appalachian League. The following year he led the league in stolen bases with 52. While a player, Trivette also managed the Chiefs for the '39 and '40 seasons.

Bernie Webb

Bernie Webb from the Poplar Ridge community attended Mary Hughes High School during the 1930's. Webb dominated in high school, where he was named as the quarterback on the all-time all-Mary Hughes football team. He then took his expertise to Milligan College where he played football and baseball. After college Webb played three years of minor league baseball. After service in WW II, he returned home to become a professional umpire in the Appalachian League. Coach Webb later taught and coached at Blountville High School for twenty years where he served as head basketball coach. He compiled a record of 313 wins and 308 losses, winning three Upper Lakes Conference Championships along the way. In 1968 he became Athletic Director at the then new Sullivan Central High School and served at that position until 1995. In 1994 Webb was inducted into both the Milligan College and Northeast Tennessee Sports Hall of Fame.

Duard Walker

Duard Walker like many other star athletes of the '30's and '40's in Piney Flats took their athletic ability to Milligan

College. Before attending Milligan, Walker served in the U.S. Navy for three years during WW II, participating in both the battles of Iwo Jima and Okinawa.

Walker graduated from Milligan in 1948 and earned his teachers license from Columbia University in 1949. For two years he taught and coached at Knox Farragut High School in Knox County, Tennessee. In 1951 Walker began his tenure at Milligan. For the next 50 years he served as a professor in the Health and P.E. Dept, coached baseball (7 years), basketball (15 years), cross-country (15 years), track and field (20 years), and served as Athletic Director for more than 40 years. In addition to these impressive credentials, Coach Walker was a Senior Olympic participant in badminton. Sports Illustrated featured him in an article in 2000 covering his many years of service in athletics. In 1993 Coach Walker was inducted into the Milligan College Sports Hall of Fame and in 1995 he was named to the Northeast Tennessee Sports Hall of Fame.

Steve Lacy

Coach Steve Lacy was a teacher and coach at Mary Hughes High School in the 1930's. It was he who started the football program at the high school by borrowing equipment from his alma mater Milligan College. Coach Lacy has been named to both the Northeast Tennessee and Milligan College Sports Halls of Fame. The Steve Lacy Field House at Milligan College is named in his honor for the legendary coach of Mary Hughes High School's first football team.

Dwight Mason

Coach Dwight Mason was Mary Hughes High School's head basketball coach for 12 years. During that time he won almost 200 games and brought home two Upper Lakes Conference Championships. Coach Mason made basketball in Piney Flats and Mary Hughes a way of life during the 1950's and 60's. His intimidating presence and intense coaching style made him one of the most respected coaches in all of East Tennessee. All total, 12 years at Mary Hughes and 2 years at Sullivan East, Coach Mason won 244 games and lost 174. He served as teacher, coach, and principal in Sullivan County for over thirty years. After retirement Coach Mason served as County Commissioner for Sullivan County for 5 years until illness forced him out of office. In 1997 Mary Hughes School named the gymnasium the "Dwight Mason Gymnasium" in his honor, finally paying the respect that was long over due. Coach Mason's legacy will always live on throughout the school and community where he gave so much joy to the people.

John McKamey

Coach John McKamey is one of the most successful men ever to attend Mary Hughes High School. In 1960 Coach McKamey became head baseball coach at Mary Hughes and served as at that position both there and at Sullivan East High School until 1987. In all Coach McKamey won over 300 games and claimed 4 conference championships. He made the program at Sullivan East one of the most respected programs in East Tennessee. For his contributions, the field at Sullivan East in named in his

119

honor. Aside from teaching and coaching, Coach McKamey has served as Sullivan County Commissioner (1976-1990, 2000-present) and as Sullivan County Executive (1990-1994). Coach McKamey has and continues to serve Piney Flats as well as anyone in the great history of Piney Flats.

Bill Wilson

Bill Wilson was one of the most feared basketball players in East Tennessee while he played at Mary Hughes. In the 1961-62 season Wilson lead the league in scoring averaging 21.6 points per game. He had a career total of 1611 points while at Mary Hughes. Wilson played one season at University of Tennessee and three seasons at East Tennessee State University, where he was team captain. Coach Wilson served as a graduate assistant at E.T.S.U. for one season and was head basketball coach at Sullivan East for 6 seasons. Coach Wilson served as a teacher, coach, and principal for over thirty years. His final year he served as head principal at Sullivan East.

Ernie Wolfe

Ernie Wolfe is arguable one of the greatest basketball players ever to play at Mary Hughes. His style of play was years ahead of his time. In an era (1961-64) when the two handed set shot was being used, Wolfe would glide through the air and create shots that people in the Rucker League of New York City would have been proud of. Wolfe is the all-time leading scorer in Mary Hughes High School history, with a grand total of 1619 points. In the '62-'63 and '63-'64 seasons Wolfe led the Upper Lakes Conference in scoring averaging 22 and 24 points respectively a game. Wolfe also set the single game scoring record with a 45-point outburst in one game. These stats are even more impressive considering there was no three-point line in Tennessee high school basketball until 1987-88 seasons. Ernie Wolfe will always be regarded as one of the best basketball players in an area where basketball is lived not just played.

Mark Mason

Mark Mason, son of Dwight Mason, is considered the measuring stick for all would be a basketball player from Mary Hughes. Mason was an outstanding basketball player at Mary Hughes and Sullivan East, where he still holds several records. He holds the record for points in a season, single season free throw percentage, and career free throw percentage. His senior season at East, his team won the schools first and only conference championship. Mason's jersey #22 has been enshrined in the schools gymnasium. From high school he played one season at E.T.S.U. and three seasons at Carson- Newman College. It was at Carson-Newman that Mason blossomed into one of the greatest basketball players ever in East Tennessee being named to the All-Conference, All-District 24, and honorable mention All-American teams. Mason was invited to a try out with the Indiana Pacers, but he had all ready begun his teaching/coaching career. Mason continued his career in basketball as a coach. He coached two seasons at Knox Carter High School in Knoxville and 9 seasons at Sullivan East. Today Mason travels the country conducting shooting clinics for elementary teams to major college teams.

121

Rick Trivett

Basketball and Baseball- Rick is the son of Hall of Famer Claude Trivett. Rick was an outstanding high school athlete at Mary Hughes from 1963-1967. Trivett played and excelled at both baseball and basketball in high school. He took his talents to Lincoln Memorial University where he was an All-Conference, All-District 24, and Honorable Mention All-American selections in Basketball and Baseball.

David Tipton

Track and Field- David went to Sullivan East from Mary Hughes and was an outstanding track star. He set the school high jump record that lasted for over twenty years. He continued his talents in track at E.T.S.U.

Dave Mason

Basketball- One of the Mason brothers that brought basketball to a new level in Piney Flats. Dave played at Sullivan East High School, but blossomed as a basketball player in college. He played two seasons at Hiwassee Junior College and transferred to Tennessee-Wesleyan where played two more seasons. At TN Wesleyan, he was an all-conference guard. After college he began a successful coaching career in both the boys and girls basketball at Gate City High School.

Ken Brown

Basketball- Ken played at Mary Hughes thru the ninth grade and then went to Science Hill High School where he played basketball. From Science Hill, Ken went on to play at Tusculum College where he became an all-conference player for the pioneers.

John Mason

Basketball- The youngest of the Mason family, John is one of the leading scorers in Sullivan East High History. After high school, John played two seasons at Hiwassee Junior College and transferred to King College for his final two seasons.

Krista Ivester (Hare)

Track and Field- 1986 TSSAA State High Jump Champion and 1987 TSSAA State Runner-Up in the high jump. Competed in four events in the Tennessee State Track and Field Championship in 1987; high jump, long jump, 800 meter relay, and 400 meter relay. The *Times News* Relay's Krista Hare Outstanding Field Events Award honors the most outstanding female field events winner. Attended Middle Tennessee State University from 87-90' where she was a member of the Ohio Valley Conference indoor championship team and the OVC High Jump Champion.

Sara Carr

Basketball- In 1985 she played for the only basketball championship team Mary Hughes has had since it became a K-8 school. Sara had a very successful career at Sullivan East High School her teams won two conference championships and at one time she held the Tennessee State record for most three point shots made in both girls and boys basketball.

Kim Bright (Peer)

Basketball- Also played for the '85 championship team at Mary Hughes and the Sullivan East championship teams in the late 1980's. She had a successful collegiate career at Milligan College where she played four years. She is now the head girl's basketball coach for the Bristol Tennessee High School Lady Vikings.

Hank Hare

Basketball- All Conference basketball player at Sullivan East High School. Scored over 1,200 points in college while attending Bristol University 89', Northland Pioneer Junior College 90-91, and Trevecca Nazerene University 91-93. He was an Academic All-American in 1991. The Hank Hare Scholar Athlete Award is given to an outstanding student-athlete at Northland Pioneer Junior College in Holbrook, Arizona. Hank is the current boys basketball coach and assistant principal at Mary Hughes Middle School. His 2002 team set the new wins record for basketball since consolidation

Andy Hare

Baseball- Three-time All-Region and All-Conference selection at Sullivan East High School and school's all-time hits leader. Three-time team captain at Milligan College and All- Tennessee Virginia Athletic Conference, TVAC, selection for the 98 season. Played at ETSU 94-95, Milligan College 95-98.

Andy Wilhoit

Baseball- All Region and All Conference selection at Sullivan East High School. Played collegiate at King College, (96-98, 99-01) where he was a two-time All-TVAC selection at third base.

Becky Sells

Basketball- All time points and rebound leader at Sullivan East High School, and named to the All-State team as a senior. At Milligan College (96-00), she became the all time points and rebound leader and was named to the All-TVAC, All Mid-South Region, and All-American teams.

Brian Mason

Basketball Coaching- Brian Mason is the son of Dwight Mason and the current principal at Mary Hughes Middle School. Brian has devoted over twenty years to Mary Hughes athletics either as a player or a coach. Mason played basketball at Mary Hughes Junior High and Sullivan East High School. He played one season collegiate at

Hiwassee Junior College. Mason later became a teacher and coach at Mary Hughes Middle School in the early 1980's. While there he coached the 1985 Girls Basketball County Championship team.

*It is difficult to give proper recognition to all those that have been selected to this Hall of Fame. Many records are incomplete, destroyed, or unknown. It is hard to make selections based solely on word of mouth. I feel that these selected are the most qualified selections. Also this is not an official Hall of Fame, it is the opinion of this writer of athletes that met the criteria that was set. In order to have an official Hall of Fame the effort of the community would be needed to provide viable information and unbiased selections.

Chapter
Seven

Miscellaneous

There are hundreds of other fascinating stories to Piney Flats, more than my mind can hold. That is why it is vital to preserving our future. We must share our stories and pass them along to the next generations. If we do not then our past will undoubtedly be forgotten.

The next few lines are dedicated to other "fun facts" that describes the story of Piney Flats. Bits and pieces of our past that will help you see where I grew up.

Piney Flats consisted of two groups of people in its early days, large landowners and slaves. Prior to the Civil War, slavery was heavily relied upon. When the War broke out may in this area were Pro-Confederate. With most of East Tennessee aiding the Union, Sullivan County was referred to as "Little Dixie." However, even with War over, a strong Confederate mentality remained, with many of the men in the 1930's being active members of the Ku Klux Klan.

After the Civil War, tenant farmers were used in place of slaves. They would work the farms and eventually save enough money to purchase a small farm for them.

In the early days of Piney Flats men were men and women were women. They were rugged and individualistic, yet very close knit with other people in the community. They believed that if you work together society would be a better place. Everyone was welcomed in each other's home. Their doors were always open and no one locked their doors at night. There was no need to. Everyone trusted each other.

All the men carried guns and it became a matter of pride who was the best shot. Shooting contests were performed frequently to determine who the best shot in the community was. The young men knew that this would be a way of earning their manhood and respect from other in the area.

From the late 1960's to 1980 the Piney Flats Ruritan sponsored horse shows at Ned King's farm. These shows would bring in visitors from all around. These shows are some of my earliest memories growing up. I remember the long caravan of participants that would make the turn up Ned King Road. We would set at my grandparent's house and wave at the endless line of wagons that made their way to the corral. It was an impressive site watching the beautiful horses prancing around the corral as hundreds of people looked on. It acted as a way to bring people together throughout the community.

In the late 1950's a proposition was made to the citizens of Piney Flats to build a racetrack. The members of the local churches met this with much resistance for they feared it would bring in drunkenness and violence to the community. As a result, the track was built about seven miles north of Piney Flats and today known as the Bristol Motor Speedway, home of the worlds fastest half-mile.

Eli Anderson first purchased the Cedar Lawn Farm, which has been in operation for well over 140 years. The significance of the farm is not it's age; it is how the money was made to purchase it. Like many people throughout the United States, Eli went to California hoping to strike it rich in the great Californian gold rush of 1849. As a result of his efforts, he did just that. Thus bringing his new fortune back home where he purchased the farm, which remains in the family to this day.

H.H. Hughes won first place at the 1933-1934 Chicago World's Fair for wheat that he grew.

Boys Scout Troop 4 is one of the oldest scout troops in East Tennessee. It began in Piney Flats in the late 1940's and has remained active to this day. Through its years, the troop has provided a great many services to the region while teaching hundreds of young men valuable life skills necessary to become a productive citizen. One of my greatest individual accomplishments was achieving the rank of Eagle Scout. I am one of over a dozen recipients of this award from Troop 4.

Writer Henry Hampton Hyder, born in 1825, resided in Piney Flats and published two stories; "The Double Golden Chains With Blazing Diamonds Strung," published in 1889 `and "The Lovers Dream" published in 1894. The earlier of the two stories is on the shelves of the Library of Congress in Washington D.C.

Sources:

Bluff City United Methodist Church, Council on Ministries. *Scenes From The Bluffs: A Pictorial History of Bluff City and Piney Flats, Tennessee.* Madison, TN: Madison Print Shop, 1976.

Mason, Becky. *Piney Flats: Past to Present.* 1997.

Conclusion

I know that there are many stories yet to be told and events that happened in Piney Flats other than those that are contained in this book. However, that is the joy of history. Everyday something new from the past always seems to raise its head to remind us of times forgotten. It is so important in preserving our heritage that we listen to our past. We need to talk to our grandparents and senior citizens and learn from the lives they lived. If we continue to ignore what they have to say, an entire era of history will be lost. Once you look back in time, today will be more appreciated.

This story of Piney Flats is one that has occurred throughout our country. Progress and small towns do not mix. Everyday another piece of small town America is falling along the wayside. It seems like that you could combine progress and maintain a close community. However, we are too busy, not educated enough, to self-centered, to career-minded, less family-minded, and too tired to focus on community issues. It is not the "in" thing to do. Unfortunately, we are missing the forest for the trees and generation after generation will never know what it is like to be part of anything. Instead our young people are being filled full of propaganda about how you must take care of yourself and not worry about anyone else. How sad. They will never know what it is like to have the warm comfort of a family-based community. Now we live in beautiful houses with other beautiful houses all around, but do not know who live in them. We do not even get to enjoy our own houses that we pay four digits a month for. In most homes in America, both husband and wife work full-time. We have to work overtime or work on holidays for double-time. After a hard days work, we pick the kids up from daycare, we pick up some carryout, throw a video in after diner to keep the kids occupied, while one spouse does housework the other gets on-line and chats with people until it's time to go to bed. That is the community of today. We have all the toys: nice houses, fancy cars, and all the latest technologies. But we do not know our neighbors or who our children's teachers are.

I am not casting stones, instead I am confessing. I am as guilty as anyone at committing these sins against a community. However, like all sin we can be forgiven. We can make an effort to preserve our communities and give our children a place to grow up in with an identity. It can't be done alone. It has to be a combined effort by all of us.

If you want to see the last bastion of community pride in Piney Flats, go to a Mary Hughes Middle School basketball game. While you are there, look around and see the people. They are excited and proud to watch their community being represented. It is an amazing site to see the Dwight Mason Gymnasium packed to standing room only. When I go to watch the Lion's play I am given hope that one day Piney Flats will be great again. There is a spark in that old gym that takes me back to a nostalgic time when the Mary Hughes Lions were not only the kings of the basketball court, but Piney Flats was the king of small town America. There is still pride in this community inside of each of us; we just have to remember what it feels like.

Hopefully the next time you drive around your community or town you might look at it in a different light and recognize the significance of those that came before you. Every town has a history but not all of them have a future. Learn your town's story and pass it on to the next generation.

Today when I drive through the many winding roads of Piney Flats, I respect the hard work and efforts of those that came before me and thank them for giving me such a great place to grow up.

Andrew D. Hare

Bibliography

Bluff City United Methodist Church, Council on Ministries. <u>Scenes From the Bluffs: A Pictorial History of Bluff City and Piney Flats, Tennessee.</u> Madison, TN: Madison Print Shop 1976.

Cox, Eugene and Joyce, <u>A History of Washington County, Tennessee</u>. Johnson City, TN: Overmountain Press, 2001.

Holston Territory Genealogical Society. <u>Families and History of Sullivan County, Tennessee Volume One 1779-1992</u>. Waynesville, NC: Walsworth Publishing, 1992.

Hyatt, Lester. "Piney Flats Just Ain't the Same Since They Torn the Depot Down." <u>Scenes From the Bluffs: A Pictorial History of Bluff City and Piney Flats, Tennessee</u>. Bluff City United Methodist Church, Council on Ministries. 1976.

Jenkins, Henry. <u>Northeast Tennessee Baseball Our Professional Players.</u> 1998.

——————————. <u>Northeast Tennessee High School Basketball Record Book</u>. 1997.

Massengill, E. Samuel. <u>The Massengills, Massengales, and Variants 1472-1931</u>. Bristol, TN: The King Printing Company, 1931.

New Bethel Presbyterian Church. <u>The New Bethel Bicentennial 1782-1982</u>. Johnson City, TN: Overmountain Press, 1996.

New Bethel Presbyterian Church. <u>The New Bethel Sesqusentinnial 1782-1932.</u> Bristol, TN: King Printing, 1932.

Piney Flats United Methodist Church. <u>History of Piney Flats United Methodist Church.</u> 1983.

Rothrock, Mary U. <u>This Is Tennessee</u>. Knoxville, TN: M.U. Rothrock, 1969.

Sakowski, Carolyn. <u>Touring The East Tennessee Backroads</u>. Winston-Salem, N.C. John F. Blair Publisher, 1993.

Spoden, Muriel C. <u>Historic Sites of Sullivan County</u>. Kingsport, TN: Kingsport Press, 1976.

Taylor, Oliver. <u>Historic Sullivan</u>. 1909. Reprinted. Johnson City, TN Overmountain Press, 1996.

<u>The Baseball Encyclopedia</u>. New York: Macmillan Publishing Co., 1993.

Torbett, Michael. "History." <u>Scenes Form the Bluff: A Pictorial History of Bluff City and Piney Flats, Tennessee</u>. Bluff City United Methodist Church, Council of Ministries. 1976.

Interviews

McKamey, John. Personal Interview. 2 July 2001.

Mason, Mark. Personal Interview. 20 October 2001.

Taylor, Lelia. Recorded Interview, "Early School Days at Mary Hughes School." 29-31 November 1987 and 1-3 December 1987.

Walker, Duard. Personal Interview. 20 October 2001.

Essays

Anderson, J.A. "Historical Dates and Items of Interest on Mary Hughes School, and Town, and Community at Large." 1945.

Starnes, Nell. "Mary Hughes Parent Teachers Association." 1953.

Taylor, Lelia. "Piney Flats." 1978.

Unpublished Documents

Mary Hughes Homecoming. 1986.

Mason, Becky. Piney Flats: Past to Present. 1997.

Profile

Andrew Donald Hare's passion for his community entered him into the challenge of researching the history of Piney Flats. He has lived in and around Piney Flats his entire life and it was his experiences growing up in this community that spurred his desire to preserve the amazing history of his home. Andrew has been involved as a leader in his community for many years. He is the Youth Director at New Bethel Presbyterian Church, as a member of Boys Scout Troop 4 he received the rank of Eagle Scout, and is a Past-President of the Piney Flats Ruritan Club. Since graduating from Milligan College, where he was a standout baseball player, Andrew has been a high school history teacher and coach since 1999.

Andrew D. Hare

Book Summary

Come See Where I Grew Up, is the collection of many years of stories, facts, and memories that have been put together to tell the history of Piney Flats, Tennessee. The book is divided into seven chapters each portraying a different image of the whole picture of this once productive and thriving community. From the Colonial era to the present day, *Come See Where I Grew Up*, covers the significant events that occurred in Piney Flats and explains how they help shape the history of the region, state, and nation.

Come See Where I Grew Up, was written with one thing in mind, and that was the preservation of our past. It is this books goal that some people may be inspired by its words enough to make a conscious effort in preserving their communities past. Every community has a history but more and more of them do not have a future. By forgetting our past, the future will be a dull place and our communities will be forgotten.

So I invite you to "come see where I grew up," and learn the history of my community.

Andrew D. Hare

About the Author

Andrew Donald Hare's passion for his community entered him into the challenge of researching the history of Piney Flats. He has lived in and around Piney Flats his entire life and it was his experiences growing up in this community that spurred his desire to preserve the amazing history of his home. Andrew has been involved as a leader in his community for many years. He is the Youth Director at New Bethel Presbyterian Church, as a member of Boys Scout Troop 4 he received the rank of Eagle Scout, and is a Past-President of the Piney Flats Ruritan Club. Since graduating from Milligan College, where he was a standout baseball player, Andrew has been a high school history teacher and coach since 1999.

www.ingramcontent.com/pod-product-compliance
Lightning Source LLC
Chambersburg PA
CBHW020441290526
45785CB00002B/961